THE BODY IS A TEMPORARY GATHERING PLACE

Andrew Bertaina

autofocus books
Orlando, Florida

©Andrew Bertaina, 2024
All rights reserved.

Published by Autofocus Books
autofocuslit.com

Essays/Literature
ISBN: 978-1-957392-30-1

Cover Illustration ©Amy Wheaton
Library of Congress Control Number: 2024931870

THE BODY IS A TEMPORARY GATHERING PLACE

Table of Contents

I

A Plane Crashes Out Over the Atlantic..................7
A Field of White..................9
An Impressionist Sketch of a Saturday Afternoon..................15
The Thin Ribbon..................21
Time Passses: On Unfinished Things..................29
Departures..................41

II (After Montaigne)

On Trains..................51
On Eating Animals..................63
On Uncertainty..................73
On Being 35..................87
On Showering and Mortality..................93
On Kissing..................97
On Baths..................107

III

This Essay Is About Everything..................125
Home Burial..................145
The Leopard..................159

I

A Plane Crashes Out Over the Atlantic

We were sitting on the shores of the Atlantic, waiting for the wind to change and the black flies to get blown back out to sea, when the plane went down. Someone near us said they saw it, single-engine, single-wing, nose-diving eight blocks from where we were, about a half-mile out to sea. For a while, like most people witnessing an accident secondhand, we speculated about causes, heart attack, engine failure, etc. Then we said what everyone says in these types of situations: that someone who was once alive was now dead, how you can't take anything for granted, life's pitch and yaw, and then the children started running too close to the water, and we had to leave off and scold them to keep them from being carried away by the waves.

Strictly speaking, I didn't participate in the conversation, though I listened as intently as you can while reading and suffering in the glare of the afternoon sun. I was reading an essay from *The Histories* by Herodotus, which deals with the rise and fall of the great Persian empire under Cyrus and Darius, and their eventual failure to conquer the Greek city states Athens and Sparta, the forebears to Rome and thus, in the mind of many Americans, us. The failure to conquer the city states was titanic enough to have a movie about it called *300*, and then the *300* workout, a series of exercises designed to give you a body made of steel, which is, if you think about it, as big as a historical event can get.

The sun was partially obscured behind faint black clouds, hung across the sky like clothes on some infinitely long blue line. I was reading the book and keeping my own private conversation, as we all do. I thought about the 6,000 Persians who died in the war and how much greater that number was than the one person on a plane falling off the coast of the living into some deeper water.

I read an article recently that said our ambitions and desires begin to keep pace somewhere around the age of 60, which means I have a lot of suffering ahead. The real reason the Persian Empire collapsed was that the scope of their ambition outpaced the means of achieving its fruition. In short, that oldest of human sins, pride—the same sin that caused the expulsion from Eden and that melted the wings of Icarus. We are not gods, or demi-gods. Though we can fly, we are destined to fall.

After a while, the sun moved imperceptibly in the sky, and we told the kids to stop throwing sand into the ocean, to stop screaming when it washed up around their small feet. On the beach, my youngest lay asleep, six months old, small chest gliding almost imperceptibly up and down. The difference between breathing and not breathing feels so slim when children are young.

I understand the difference between the plane and the book. The plane happened now, or moments ago, and whatever happened to Cyrus and Darius and thousands of Persians happened roughly 2,000 years ago, which allows those deaths, those bones, time enough to sink in. This fall was a new one. And though there will be no history 2,000 years hence of this particular day, I will retain, somewhere in the stray matter of my brain, the memory of the image of a plane going down, of the cold water touching my bare feet. The youngest is rolling around on the blanket. It is time for us, still kicking and screaming, to go home.

A Field of White

On one of those rare mornings when I'm alone, not haggling over Cheerios and milk, stuffing kids into coats and hats before haul-assing out the door to drop them at school and buzzing across town to my own job, I drink coffee. And with the ceramic cup, designed with swaths of red and orange to mimic the landscape of the desert southwest, warming my hands, I look out the window as little non-descript birds hop about on the grass, eating worms or pecking furtively at bits of trash. Acorns are strewn across the yard, muddied by melting snow. The skeletal remains of last year's indigo patiently await their resurrection.

My daughter, age five, has asked me to set up tea time. She is not patient. The stuffed bear looks restless as well, slouched drunkenly in a small wicker chair.

Oh, what a waste I make of time. I'll sit by the window for longer than I intended, whittling down the minutes and hours of the day, dreaming of writing. Instead of writing, though, I think, which is so much easier than piecing words together. Thoughts are allowed to fold and unfold. You needn't mold them into a pleasing shape like you must with narrative. And thus, they often feel complete. Writing into your idea is like tapping at the edge of a very still pond and watching the ripples go, arcs of silver bending across the once placid surface. I have another sip of coffee as the orange light of an early morning sun sets the oaks' bark briefly afire.

We're using the Plan Toys tea set, which means the tea bags are wooden blocks with pieces of string affixed to the top. In truth, I've had better tea. She claps her hands when she gets excited.

Most days I work late and arrive home with the fan whirring upstairs, thick white noise blanketing their small bodies, curved in geometries of sleep. I usually write in the evenings. Though by usually, I mean rarely, or sometimes but not often.

Finally I have time and quiet to work. But first I check Facebook and my e-mail, yearning for some distraction, a reminder like a postcard that someone is thinking of me, or has tucked me away in the drawer of their mind. There is an unquiet place within me that longs so deeply for connection, for affirmation, I'll stare at the screen or message everyone I know, desperate to catch someone in the web of my thoughts, in the portrait of my day. And I scroll and scroll through updates and ads, children at war in Africa, Republican politics, microaggressions, pictures of dinners, of weddings, of cats on desks.

She's very meticulous about the tea, matching each small saucer on each plate, handling them with intense care. "Daddy," she yells. "We need sugar." The stuffed bear looks obese, but I don't ask after Splenda.

And like a passing cloud, hung on the curtain of the sky, my time floats away. Soon enough the children will be asking me to peel oranges, to pour milk, to build tracks, to give them pieces of my day. I had an idea for a short story, though I often think I should strictly write essays, their looping form and digressions are a better stylistic fit for my impatient brain—a vessel easily blown off course. Or it may be that I only think I'm better at essays, but am not, in fact, any better at essays. Or maybe other people think I'm better at essays. Or maybe I just think that people think I'm better at essays because I've misconstrued a comment or two. Or perhaps I am right in believing people think I am better at essays, but they are wrong because I am not, in fact, better at essays. I am often confused.

I am wearing a small silver tiara and asking for sugar.

The idea was to have a linked set of stories based on math problems. The mathematical problems would hold the story together like ties to a rail. But now I am writing an essay about not writing these short stories, so maybe even the mathematical foundation is unsound, or proof of my errors in logic. Proof is a math joke.

The tea is never warm at these gatherings of porcelain dolls and stuffed bears named Apples.

I had an idea for a story about a village where it starts raining pictures. I think Dutch Golden Age, classical realism raised to the nth degree suddenly hailing down on a remote village from a Rembrandt-inspired sky, puffs of grey clouds limned by shards of golden-hued light, a farmer looking up from his work. I don't know if the story was going to focus on what was in the pictures, the contrasts Rembrandt created between brown Dutch villages and the background of clouds and mountains, or his fine use of chiaroscuro, or whether it was going to focus on the faces and dispositions of the villagers, scattering about the village, running for their life as Vermeer's *Officer and Laughing Girl* careens toward them, the girl in the picture, usually so timid-looking in her maid's hat, terrifying as she falls.

No one at the table is passing the cream. The conversation is as wooden as the tea, I say, but no one laughs.

I have a problem of late, which is that all my ideas for stories are just that, ideas alone, jars unopened on the dusty shelves of my mind. And all my ideas for essays are about riding on trains or not writing essays. Sometimes, when I'm standing in line at the grocery store, basket full of Persian cucumbers, baby carrots, and enough apples to feed a barbarian horde, I'll have an idea hit like a lightning strike, and I'll start working out intricate details in my head, precise plot points, ashy clouds, the lips of a girl, or ways an essay can begin to take shape around a simple idea. But I never have a pen. And by the time I've loaded up the groceries, driven across town, read *Frog and Toad*, tucked the children into bed and watched an episode of *Mad Men*, I'll have forgotten that brilliant strike amidst the crush of the day. And so thoughts slip away like bits of smoke into the blued evening.

The half-light of the lamp gives the bear a slightly sinister look and the girl doesn't seem to notice at all, pouring tea willy-nilly for everyone.

What if people start seeing pictures of themselves falling from the sky? Or moments that they'd otherwise like to keep hidden? Is it religious, then, or a cosmic joke, this plague of paintings? Maybe it should be raining postcards. The postcards would say things like this:

I am living now in a cottage in England where my dog has just died. I know you won't be reading this until after you return. Antarctica is so far away. I wanted to tell you about the red buds on the tree, the rain cutting through the sky and fields of grass that moved like water, dusky pillars of autumnal light that fell across damp floors, spinning out the mysterious day in which we are both present and absent, you somewhere at the back of a ship, eating a can of beans, and me, strangely still here, telling you of my dead dog as though you can know, as though you will care. I cannot write about anything else but the strangeness of life, how a bulb should turn into a purple flower, does it not sometimes strike you as immensely silly? When I am really writing, I suppose I feel less lonely, and I wrap up these letters and lay them out on the dresser as if you will return.

Sometimes I open up old documents on the computer to see if I used to be a good writer, or if I've grown, or if I've remained static. In truth, I can't tell if the work is any better. Taste is subjective and what pleased me at twenty-five may not please me at thirty-two, but I have to admit that the writing has remained the same, and it is I who have changed. In short, I don't know. This is also a short and unsatisfying answer for most of the questions in the universe.

The tea party is over now and no one, especially not the one-eyed doll, is making a move to clean up. It looks like it falls to me.

The sun has been down for hours now. Phosphorescent lamps in the alley cast halos on the oak tree in our yard, giving it a ghoulish pallor, reticulate branches lifting skyward as if casting a spell. And I haven't written a damn thing. Or only this damn thing, which isn't really a thing at all. It's a mess. Everything is always a mess—the universe, afternoons by the pool, hairstyles, relationships, they all tend toward disorder, and one must always be sweeping or dusting, or making lists, or love, or being productive in order to make sense of it. Entropy reigns. If the universe were orderly, this essay would not be a random collection of thoughts, ephemera spun out from an ephemeral and contingent creature. Instead, it would read like a math theorem or a series of syllogisms; "the world is all that is the case," though Wittgenstein probably meant universe.

It's late now, which means that the time to turn this into something coherent has passed. A squirrel roots around inside our walls, making a nest to keep warm, creating a parallel between us, as I work with the warm computer in my lap, in a nest of blankets. I suppose I could give this essay something more coherent like a mathematical notation, or a refrain about a tea party, something to hold it together. But then I'd be going to bed at 12:44am or 1:17am, and the children wake so early. And if I go to bed too late I will be tired at work, and tired at home, and I will fall asleep at 8:30pm, or yell at my wife and children, telling them how my life is so tiring and how I can't get a damn thing done, and then I will nap, and then it will take me a while to go to sleep, and I will stay up until 12:37am trying to write and failing once again. If only Shakespeare hadn't written the sonnets, perhaps I could sleep well, knowing that man can only do so much in a lifetime. I creep upstairs and kiss the children on their foreheads, peaceful for a moment, in the quiet of sleep.

The dolls are sitting in the dark, waiting for the next tea party to begin, with the patience of statues, of portraits on the walls of museums.

And time continues to be whittled away, carving away at me as well, hollowing out my insides, making its way toward bone. A cold wind rattles the panes where I peer out into the darkness, this time seeing not a damn thing. Just shades of more darkness, which doesn't allow me to paint any picture at all. Leaving you instead with this soft patter of words amidst the thousands you'll see today, an impression only, like that of a single snowflake on a field of white.

An Impressionist Sketch of a Saturday Afternoon

Most mornings I'm stretched thin from watching the children, two and four, playing cars, playing instruments, playing at fire truck puzzles, playing with time that I've tried to squirrel away for writing, for thinking, for reading. Though what that time really amounts to is sitting on the couch with an issue of *Harper's* in a state of very mild depression at the state of the world, the country, the shape of life. Now I rarely write or think or read. But I've gotten quite good at sorting out the edge pieces of puzzles, quite good at doing noises of bears roaring and sea lions grunting and quite good at vrooming cars across the hardwood floor, sending them careening off the wall and into the kitchen, scurrying like mice, like time, madcapping across the floor like the weeks and months of winter passing.

When we first moved into our house, a squirrel used to wake us Saturday mornings, hammering acorns into the attic floor where he'd pile them in preparation for the cold winter to come as I tried to squirrel away time to sleep after a late-night writing yet another story for my graduate school class in which two people, usually married, were not getting along. The divorce rate in novels is staggering.

I don't know that I'd ever have had children if not for my wife, who is a planner: meals, trips to the grocery store, trips to museums, totes for winter clothes, and children, which is not to say that I do not love the children or can imagine the world without them. But rather, that though I am an inconsistent person, often subject to change like a tree's leaf blowing in the wind, I am not sure if I ever would have geared myself up for children—for naps and diapers, for the boredom of a Saturday morning spent reading "Little Bo Peep" ten times in a row to a captive audience, all the while captive in my own mind, trying to be anywhere but counting sheep while simultaneously adoring the warmth coming from their small, energetic bodies, pressed against my shoulder.

But this Saturday morning I'm alone. I'm bad at being alone and have a tendency to fill my free time by calling people and making coffee dates or messaging them about their lives, their failures, or the quiet way they are spending a Tuesday. And sometimes, without a hint of irony, I spend time with those people, complaining to them that I don't have any time to myself and am forever surrounded by people. Sometimes, though not often, for we humans are narcissists, it will dawn on them that I'm spending time with them that I could be spending on my own, which I've just articulated is a problem of mine. So they will volunteer to cut things short, just a cup, just a hello, and I forestall them, ask them for another coffee or to stay through dinner, not because I am afraid of being alone but because I crave company.

Alone, I drink a large cup of coffee and watch things happen outside the window. I suspect sometimes that life is contiguous, an uninterrupted flow that is sometimes interrupted by small moments, like ripples in a river. Or perhaps, life is not discrete at all, but a series of momentary narratives surrounding big events that never happen, or are brief, like *Tristram Shandy*, a point that's always out of reach, only kept in mind. Or perhaps life is like a sculpture constructed through a series of long ropes, marriage, death, family, work, that we think hold us together, but really, beneath that, are large nets, time without definition that becomes how we spend time—a Tuesday morning commute on the train, an appointment at the dermatologist office that results in everything being just fine, the moments of boredom waiting for the doctor to enter, for the calendar to load, so you can schedule your next appointment in a year, preferably on a Tuesday, which is usually good for you. I know of very few novels about waiting for a Google calendar to load, for the kettle to warm, for the frost to melt from the windshield.

Outside my window, as I drink coffee, a small bird, a house wren perhaps, sits in the arches of a small bush, red berries of dubious edibility wreathing him, he moves sharply and quickly, bird-like is perhaps the best description. Though that's a silly way to describe a bird in the vehicle of prose, which depends on precision, like a clock, like God, like my bowels. And my description of the bird's movement as bird-like is reminiscent of a child using the word in the definition to describe the word's meaning. The column is columnar. The bird's movement is more akin to certain kinds of hip hop dancing, popping and locking, each movement designed to be at once dramatic and distinct, or an Ethiopian dance that sees the dancer simultaneously nodding their head sharply and pushing their shoulders forward in a sharp rhythm—a bird winging into flight. Though I didn't intend to write about birds at all.

High on a river of caffeine, I drove down Military, crossing Rock Creek Park. Sheaths of ivy enveloped the beech and elm, gauzy green gowns worn for a ball that's never coming. The streets were dark, washed clean by the rain, a small woman of indeterminate age waited for the bus, standing on a thin island of cement. Down the road, I turned onto a side street that cuts through the edge of the park haphazardly, full of potholes and eroding away at the edges, an old tributary of the creek repurposed to cross town, but still trying each spring, each rainstorm, to reclaim its real status. And I know, as everyone knows, that some day when we are gone, it will.

The sunlight filtered through the yellow and orange leaves of the trees, creating discontinuities, flashes of shadow and light, pattering on the car like a morality play of the human soul. When it comes to morality, or whether or not I want to be reading a children's book, I am always of two minds, in two places. It is unwise, I concluded, my mind and heart racing like a kettle drum, to drink a large cup of coffee in the morning. From there, everything became a simulacrum of the heart's fervid beat, the world flying fast and registering like an impressionist painting of light in the trees, shelves of wet leaves lining the road, houses with long wrought iron gates, ivy climbing the chimney, a library room of solid glass, a swimming pool at the edge of the park and gardeners pulling up in large trucks to take stock of all that empty space. All this making an impression upon my mind, which is bent inward and outward at once, registering as much of the world as it can contain, multitudes.

I am thinking of how my daughter, seated backwards in her toddler seat, always said, "forest," when we pass through this particular half-mile of road, and now I am thinking of her absence, and the quiet that settles over the car. I am simultaneously composing a letter to a dear friend about my inability to structure sentences properly, which also includes a disquisition on my failed attempts at writing, which includes laziness, which you can see above when I describe the birds as African dancers—a description that needs to be more finely attuned to the precise movements of their clavicles, the sharp thrust of their heads forward, veins showing through like bits of ore and the rounding of their shoulders as opposed to the rough sketch I've offered.

But I try. I try and I try. I wake early and pour cereal and give baths and even speak to the children in a British accent with a small hand puppet called Mr. Froggerton. But none of it matters because soon enough I'll be annoyed about defiance, about the pooping, all the goddamn pooping, about the lack of precision in my writing about a caffeine-infused Saturday morning.

I'm going to build a scaffold with words instead and carry you safely from sentence to sentence, from thought to thought, like a duckling walking her chicks through Boston, with transition sentences as blocky and secure as an Irish police man, guiding you along the way.

But self-castigation in writing can go on indefinitely, much like the stories in *Tristram Shandy*, but you see, I've said that before. And this is how we go round and round like the wheels on a bus, like the life of an adult, routine to routine and then suddenly you are fifty or sixty or people are gathered around your bed at a nursing home. All this thinking of children, of frogs, of solitude is happening in the car that Saturday morning while I was listening to "Someone Like You" by Adele, which reminded me that day that I am more apt to cry when I am alone for a few hours, and that, perhaps, I am a crier. Someone who finds things to weep at all the time, sad movies, the ruby red crest of sunrise on the shells of old buildings, but that I don't cry often because I'm rarely alone when I experience the world, which breaks my heart with its beauty when I'm open to it. And I am simultaneously aware that this particular song has been spoofed, quite amazingly, by SNL for its tear-inducing quality, while also thinking of the NPR story about the same subject, "Someone Like You "and tears, that identified the arpeggios as the root cause of the weepiness. Apparently, arpeggios are like funerals. The quiet therefore wasn't, true quiet, but just the silence of a child's insistent questioning. I am also kind of singing along, poorly, which is the only way I know how to sing, and I am aware that I wouldn't do it with anyone else in the car, and thinking about what that means, about our relationship to society, which dulls our singing voices and dries our tear ducts and one can hardly begin to think such things without mentioning Walden. Goddamn Walden hovering there next to Facebook and Twitter and Snapchat and all the ways that we can choose to never, thank God, be alone. I am also aware of gender norms and stereotypes around female music, and though we are a newly awakening society to the plurality of our identities, I am also vaguely wondering whether I should be enjoying the power ballad at all. Though I've loved power ballads since I was ten.

Whitney Houston and "I Will Always Love You" are threaded through my teenage years. These thoughts are all happening in roughly two to three seconds time, a rapid sort of association that makes me realize how effectively mimetic poetry can be. These brief meditations, a few seconds time remind me immediately of other things, including the wonderful short story, "Good Old Neon," by David Foster Wallace, in which he attempts to describe the brain's speed of light functioning, "What exactly do you think you are? The millions and trillions of thoughts, memories, juxtapositions — even crazy ones like this, you're thinking — that flash through your head and disappear?"

What if I told you that I am nothing at all? Or what if I told you what I told my daughter, that we're all bits of stardust? Would it change anything? So cry all you want, I won't tell anyone. Please don't tell anyone. Don't tell them a damn thing.

Shh...listen. I want both of us to strip off our clothes and to lie down on my bed, so we can listen to the cars driving past on the wintry streets below, our heads attuned, for once, to nothing but the sound of things passing.

The Thin Ribbon

The drive was nine hours long, and I was alone, which meant I was bound to start thinking about death. It's like putting a fox in a hen house, leaving me alone in a car with the specter of death. I don't know why I think about it so much when it hasn't really hit my life directly in my thirty-four years. No dead parents or siblings, just the usual passing, although I mean dying, of my grandparents, one after another, death of the elderly accumulating like a snowfall, not unexpected.

I suspect the reason that I think so much about death is that I am a rather insignificant creature, radically so, and uneasy with that reality. I suspect also that it has something to do with my loss of the faith that shepherded me through the first thirty-some-odd years of life.

Determining when I lost my faith is like determining when I found it. I don't exactly know. It faded like light from the sky. But I have not experienced this loss of faith as something enlightening, a chance to do all those things I had once thought sinful. Rather, I experience it as a loss. Where am I going when I die? I expect nowhere.

It rained over the weekend. The rivers have run over their banks, and the sluices are full of water, black mirrors echoing the sky. I started thinking then about my own death and how everyone one day is going to die and that so many had already done so, those facts, like our existence on this blip of a planet in a massive universe that slips by without notice—unless you are driving across the country. I think of the bones of the dead, shrouded in dirt, buried inside pyramids, and lain by old English countryside churches, the gravestones folding over like rotted teeth in the ground. And then, as the mind wanders, as it's prone to do, I think of my skin washed in light, standing years ago, on a hillside above one of the small towns of the Cinque Terre, on the west coast of Italy, in a cemetery that overlooked the ocean. The cemeteries on the large hillsides were ordered by Napoleon during his run through Italy. He'd feared contamination by the dead and had the cemeteries built above the towns, gifting the 180-degree views of the sea and hillsides to the dead. In Nordic culture, entire ships were buried with kings, in Egypt, full retinues, replete with mummified cats. Even Neanderthals had graves. We don't know where we go, but we've always known it's important.

I reached the clifftops after an ambling walk up a dirt road lined in flowers, then a steeper incline of stone steps, smoothed by footfalls—mausoleums, dried roses, an inscription in Italian, and, in the distance, the long, slick back of the ocean rose out to meet the neck of the horizon. I was traveling with my wife, and we bent among the tombs, reading names of people we'd never known, who never could have imagined an American couple in their mid-twenties peering down to read their names. And at that moment, the breeze on my skin, a splash of color from the town below, I felt myself briefly abiding between the eternity of the ocean and death, both seemingly limitless and deep.

I'd spent the weekend in Ann Arbor, with my brother, rooting for a football team that we'd loved for decades because in our childhood we thought they had cool helmets. The road home to Washington, D.C., spread like a ribbon across the states: Michigan, Ohio, Pennsylvania, Maryland. I grew up watching Michigan games in California, in the warmth of the Sacramento River

Valley. The same California where I remember seeing roads fluttering like ribbons, slithering above the ground as if they were alive, just after the Bay Area earthquake, though the truth is that I can't remember if it's actual footage from an earthquake that I'm conjuring up or whether it's something I've taken from a movie and repurposed into a memory. So much of our memory is like that, conjured up to fit the facts of our present moment. I can't be sure of much. Of this uncertainty, at least I can be sure.

The Pennsylvania road stretched out before me, rising and falling, wavelike in mimicry of the soft undulations of the land. At one point, this land, these hillsides had been the West, where people had settled to start families, start lives, run away from something they didn't like. Like anyone running, like me on any given day, you can't escape yourself. You are always running headlong with yourself, passing through the splashes of late-arriving sun, past the shadows of clouds, asking, is this it? Is this all there is?

I have children, five and three. Having children was not an easy decision; nor has it been easy to care for them, which has been a grinding part of my daily existence since their birth. I have swaddled them, shushed them, lain on the floor next to their crib for hours on the hardwood. I have read to them from the same damn book time and time again and sometimes stayed awake while they slept, gazing at the pale moon bobbing in the sky, not giving a damn. I have seen time inverted in my children, lived backward, as they unwittingly take moment after moment that my selfish soul tries to claim as mine, but I lie down again, I flip the page and read. The little engine can make it up the mountain, and I go on.

As I drove from highway to highway, I thought of an interview I watched with Jorge Luis Borges, in which he said that he'd like to be remembered for a short story or two, but then again, said the great Argentine writer translated into a sea of languages, we'll all be forgotten. It seems to me a terrible sentiment, made no less terrible by its veracity. In the midst of this reverie, I wondered if the car in front of me was going to slam on its brakes, or if the car next to me was going to swerve out of its lane. I wondered what death would feel like, even though I suspect the answer is nothing. In short, I wondered if I was going to die. The answer is a certainty, and yet the exact date and time are unknown. It's a surprise party at which I'm the only guest.

In the Bible, Methuselah lived almost a thousand years, Abraham for 175, Noah for 950. I don't know what any of this is supposed to mean if I don't believe in it.

Because of a poem I read the previous week, I kept thinking of rain made red by a streetlight, falling on asphalt. In the distance are a low hill sheathed in corn rows and a solitary cow, not contemplating death, lapping with quick flicks of tongue at a fissure where the water gathered and reflected the sky and that particular cow.

They say that you live on through your children, which is sort of true, gene-wise, but I suspect that something deeper is meant by that sentiment, something essential that's transmitted from you to your children. I can tell you already that I'll be gone when I'm gone, and my children will carry on as themselves, perhaps thinking of me, perhaps writing of me, but definitely as their own. My daughter, age five, already has a passionate and stubborn personality entirely of her own devising. If I still believed in such things, I'd say she was created in the image of a stubborn God.

The sun comes out eventually, which lifts my thoughts from the grave. When I was driving through parts of Pennsylvania, greener than a boy from California ever could have imagined—long tracts of unidentifiable trees lined the alluvial banks of rivers whose names I briefly saw on signs before passing over them—I started thinking of being alone. I am almost never alone. I have two children and a wife, a job, and am working on a second graduate degree. I am so afraid of being alone that I gather my friends to me like a mother hen, pulling them closer and closer. And yet, I want to live in quiet. I want to move out into the heart of the country and watch blackbirds alight in bare branches, crows in murders over fallow fields.

I wake in the mornings to requests for Cheerios and bagels with half cream cheese and half peanut butter. In the evenings, there are baths and brushings of teeth and readings of stories that my mother read to me as a child—honk honk go the ducklings, sleep sleep goes my mind, read read go the children.

On the drive there were slender spindles of road that led up from unpopulated river valleys, hinting at places unexplored. And I looked at those thin stretches of road with the same gleam that a child who has just learned of dinosaur bones looks at a rough patch of dirt. I want to go there, my heart said, as the car moved past it more quickly than I'd wish. I am thirty-four years old now, and time is passing faster and faster. In warmer months, I'd slip my arm out the window and ride the waves of wind, feeling intensely all that passes.

I kept trying to construct something meaningful out of the green hills splashed with cows, the green hills made up of greener grass, the green hills made up of deciduous trees. What is any small bit of nature made up of? Where is its meaning? Is it the trees rustling in the breeze? Is it the water pooling on the ground, falling from the sky? Look up. Is it the clouds that scuttle? Is it the small rabbits munching on tubers, or the crows that blacken a portion of this otherwise grey day? Is it the small insects, a near-infinite number that line the greened stalks of plants or that worm through soft soil? Is it any of these things? Or is the moment only composed of what I choose to take out of it—a thin strip of river that cuts like a saw through the architecture of the land, a flock of birds heading west over a grey cap of sky, the world nothing, then, but a narrow strip of my consciousness.

In the end, I have to silence my thoughts, which, once they get going, are like a freight train barreling through the night. I listened to a book on tape. I'd never read *1984*, but I listened intently to Orwell as I passed through states, valleys, and cities I'll never stop in. Being read to reminded me of my childhood, when my mother would read us to sleep, her free hand gently stroking my hair. I find comfort in listening. The words induce their own kind of silence. And my mind returned to my own children, wearing footie pajamas with trains and princesses, tucked beneath my arms, the lamplight spilling over my shoulder as I read about an engine who could.

Sometimes before the story they ask me questions.

My three-year-old, pink-cheeked and sweet, asks, "Am I going to die?" "Yes," I say.

"Am I going to die forever?" "Yes, forever," I answer. "Will I find my way back?" "No." I say.

"Is the house going to die?"

"No," I say. "The house doesn't have a soul."

Just then my daughter, freshly turned five, who has been organizing books in the next room, chimes in, "I don't want to have a soul."

The road began to narrow, and the trees diminished like light come evening. The stream of cars increased as I neared Washington, D.C., my home now these last nine years, perhaps the place that I'll die, far from the golden hills and live oaks of my California youth. But I am still relatively young now, and it's long drives that induce unquiet thoughts. I needed voices and laughter to bring me out of the shell that I'd created, that I'd walk around inside all the time if not for the lives of those near and dear to me, so brief, so luminous.

Back in the city, I took a bus to work amidst a group of students starting their freshman years in college. The sky was low, and the rain pattered against the glass, making ribbons as it slipped down the pane. The new students were excited; I could hear it in the rise and fall of their voices. And I was still locked inside myself, listening to the quiet thrum of my thoughts, carrying me down that longer road whose signposts are not always as clear. But soon enough, the day would end, and I'd be home. *Darling, come take my cold hands and press them to your stomach. I so desperately want to be warm.*

Time Passes: On Unfinished Things

I remember endless summer days as a child—days spent in blistering California heat, roaming through the grass, climbing the towering cumquat tree, holding my finger out to crickets, or letting out a long parabolic rope of pee onto the juniper. Why did the summer days—the crickets chirping, the ice clinking in a glass of lemonade—seem to distend, until they fill up large recesses of memory?

Like any good essayist, I set out to answer the question of time's riddle. Like most good questions, it turns out that the answer is multi-faceted and not entirely conclusive. The explanations range from the mathematical to the psychological and neurological. The typical hypothesis is that our young brains are rapidly encoding new experiences, every scent of a rose, every buzz of a fly has the potential to create a new memory. Just this week, my own children were shouting about a bee that had flown into the car, squirming in their seats like wild animals.

"That's not a bee," I said. "That's just a fly. And even if it was a bee, they don't bother you unless you bother them."

In my experience, the discovery of the bug would have resulted in me rolling down the window and continuing to think about the structure of my day, of logistics of the weekend. To the children, the fly was a novel experience. It wasn't even a fly. It was a havoc-causing bee.

The logarithmic explanation also explains our differing perceptions of time. The explanation runs thusly, when you are two years old, a summer is ⅛ of your lived experience. Thus, a summer, or even a day can feel like a long stretch of time relative to the total sum of your life. For an adult of forty, a summer feels like 0.00625 percent. By this explanation, which feels a bit like breaking down why a joke is hilarious and taking the piss out of it, and this essay, see line one, is pro piss, it makes sense that our experience of time as a child feels elongated and drastically truncated as we age.

The last explanation comes from a recent study at Duke University. In this study, it was found that brain degradation contributed to a perceptual difference in how the young and old experience time. Because new brains are much more efficient at processing and encoding information, there is a density to time, a rapid-fire sense that everything is happening all at once, which declines as our brains' ability to encode declines as well.

But why discuss time anyway? Isn't it the job of an essayist to bring time to life, to mention the screened-in porch, the loose fence board we all used to sneak under to travel between backyards? I don't entirely know why I'm fascinated by time. Sometimes I assume that everyone else is as baffled or interested in precisely the same sorts of things I am, but I've learned that isn't true.

What is time exactly? A difficult question, and well beyond the scope of what I intend to write as I possess no special knowledge of relativity or quantum mechanics. My investigation involves the substance of how we spend our time, ensconced at a particular moment in time in the twenty-first century. What is time? It is that which passes by in any given American urban life like mine—retrieving the children from school, passing through streams of traffic, pedestrians high-tailing it through crosswalks and bikes vaguely following the laws of traffic, the row of azaleas and coneflowers that line the mulch on my short walk to the gym. Time is that which is spent. Or perhaps spent is the wrong phrase, as though we had a choice in the matter. Time is sitting on the front porch steps, bony butt aching, while the wind rattles the limbs of a distant oak, and the children are away for the night, spending the evening with their mother. But I am also concerned with the oddities of time, the way that it wraps around a black hole, the way that it influences an essayist recording the patter of thoughts or how the impressionists recorded its passage by shifting the way that light moved through the trees.

The final score in the Oklahoma City vs. Memphis Grizzlies game was 87-81. This fact is a mooring point and perhaps why sports bring me pleasure. Sometimes I'll find myself between sentences in this essay, brain idling, living in the interstices that comprise most of our lives, and I'll click back to my prior tab, which affirms the final score of the game was 87-81. This is largely due to the compulsive way I pass time, checking and rechecking tabs on the internet, always with the nagging sense that I've missed something. I've read that the internet is addictive, in part because we are information-seeking creatures, and we've now been provided an endless repository to mine for uselessness. Implicit in the prior statement, perhaps problematically, is that our lives should have some use beyond checking the internet for basketball scores and cat memes. This implicit assumption is that our time should be spent meaningfully. Should time be spent meaningfully? And if so, why? Is it because we will all one day be gone? I am troubled by the assumption that time should be well spent because the answers have varied across cultures and time. The Spartans seemed to think it was noble, and perhaps desirable to die in war, the Buddhists in Tibet, to live and die peacefully.

Whenever I was told that I was wasting time—playing video games, watching sitcoms—I wondered what time was for. It's not as though it's a blunt instrument, not a hammer, nor a wall hanger, nor a puzzle. Its passage is inexorable, strange, and, or so it seems to me, largely contingent on the particularities of personality, identity, and the logic of the culture you belong to.

Our lives are linear, even if we don't always experience them that way. I often spend minutes in mindless reverie, imagining an e-mail I'll send to a friend I've lost touch with, all the while passing the present moment, willfully not attending to it. Even if I imagine my parallel lives, seemingly breaking the wheel of time by moving sideways or backward through it, or if I indulge in memory, my mother's fiery red hair, a day spent in childhood dropping water on a teeming mass of ants, contemporaneous time still plods inexorably forward. And all our history in time trails behind us like the contrails of a comet—broken marriages, broken fingers, broken promises, a mid-day cup of tea on the Ponte Vecchio. And perhaps that's the real answer, time is what we make of it rather than what we dream. And yet most of what I do is dream, imagine, search, as opposed to inhabit.

What is it that I think I'm missing in the current moment? Why do I keep checking the same tabs over and over, restless as the wind? Reader, I've done it just now, in the middle of this thought. Given our current understanding of time and the rules of basketball, it is unlikely that the score of the game will ever be anything but 87-81. Given my understanding of time and the rules of life, I will continue spinning through space on a giant rock, checking the internet for answers to the important questions: how the weather is in Illinois today, what the chances are for a mid-term candidate in the House, what's a good substitute for buttermilk? I can fill my time with so many questions that don't approach why I'm unhappy. I needn't ever stop long enough to ask. The present moment provides an endless distraction to the deeper questions, not a novel thought, but a salient one as I am the sort of person who prides himself on asking deeper questions and even I can barely muster up the attention span of half an hour to ponder much of anything. All the while, the fan is humming, and the children are still lodged in sleep, quiet as God. The children who never seem to need more from life than food, water, entertainment. When do human beings develop an existential nature?

I find myself, as I waste away another day on tab after tab, wondering what to do with time. Time, which can be incredibly boring, or stimulating. I can read a book, or stare blankly at a spreadsheet, but time must be passed somehow. Time is oppressive that way, pressing down on the day like gravity on the earth. Perhaps that's why so many people take pleasure in structure: having time externally defined relieves the pressure of deciding what to do with it. I too live a structured life, two jobs, two children, but I press against the hours, restless as the wind.

Beyond that, the problem of what to do with time is bourgeoise privilege. The ability to even ask the question is concomitant with that privilege. One of my favorite party anecdotes to share is how the Pirahã people of the Amazon rainforest, one of the last groups of hunter-gatherers spend their time. On average, they spend about four hours a day working and the rest is spent hanging about and exchanging jokes and stories. Would that be enough to fill the hours? Has my relatively privileged life of higher education led me to prioritize information seeking and academic achievements, which don't even make me happy? Is it plausible that my life is a waste of time?

I grew up in a religious family and was given to look for signs that portended the end of the world: Y2K, 9/11, a particularly fierce sunset. There is nothing quite like the surge of feeling that accompanies the probable end of the world, merely because the sun is flaring bright orange over a row of deciduous trees. I'd imagine the world coming to an end, Christ walking down, the heavens unfurling. Now I no longer look at the sky and wonder after glory. I wonder if the corresponding image will look good on Instagram.

I was raised in a Christian home and attended a Christian college, which means that one of the texts I've spent the most time with is the Bible. The Bible is unique in its treatment of time, cramming billions of years, the formation of planets, gases, light, and the redemption of humanity into a scant 1,200 pages. I'd have thought it would at least take 2,000. It took Proust nearly 4,500 to cover the first few decades of his life. Thus, what the Bible succeeds at is the violent compression of time, which mirrors that of our own beginning.

Though the Bible's compression is admirable, it falls egregiously short where Proust, Woolf, Joyce and others soar—in the depiction of human consciousness. The characters in the Bible are flattened by their lack of interiority. Though their duality is well-expressed. Think of David sending Bathsheba's husband off to war, so he can have her as his own. Of course, perhaps the Bible falls so far short because it isn't trying to depict consciousness. In fact, the Bible isn't a historical document either. It's a hodgepodge of different styles, poetry, fable, metaphorical, practical instruction, hallucinatory apocalypse, and the stoic tract of Ecclesiastes.

But I fear that an essay that goes on too long about the Bible runs the risk of overstaying its welcome. I think that the majority of the times I've been drowsy beyond human comprehension has been during overlong sermons. Structurally, the early portions of the Bible rely on parataxis, events are called into life and responded to. Be light; there was light. This structure mimics our lives, though admittedly, the scale is a bit different, universe and light switch.

In our lives, events unfold like leaves falling from an autumnal tree, one after another. As I noted above, even if we fight this linear reality with stories, jokes, narrative tricks, time still marches forward. We can write a book that moves backward, but we can't do anything but hurtle forward ourselves. Who hasn't felt that life is sometimes this way? As though the rush of days flows past us without the time for us to ever apply meaning? The human mind can only hold an experience in active memory for three seconds before it is filed away or lost to the great empty recess of forgotten things that comprise most of our lives, like the dark matter that holds together the universe.

Crucially though, the difference between Biblical time and my current understanding of time is that we are not moving toward anything at all, while the Bible sends the reader moving toward Christ. Thus, lives and linear time should be compressed in order to apply the structural integrity, alpha and omega. Meanwhile, as Proust knows, if all we have is the here and now, and we move toward nothing determinate, then why not expand the details, imbue the ordinary life with rich sensory detail, the fiery red sunset, the blooming jacaranda.

Unlike my religious upbringing, I think we just move, not with intent, toward either a Big Crunch, pure compression or toward the Big Rip, a universe too large to sustain anything.

The Bible also mirrors our lives by decentering human experience. Not that we consider our lives decentered. In fact, as everyone who has access to the internet has already noted, social media amplifies our belief that we are at the center of the universe. Like Jesus, but without the sandals and crucifixion. But the Bible, like the ocean or the sky, reminds us that our lives are insignificant, and if the Renaissance was about the flourishing of human grandeur, the Industrial Revolution and the growth of capitalism has been about the flourishing of technologies, capital, and structures that are beyond human control. Our lives are already shaped, as though by God, by the cultural forces into which we are born. And, in a way, our lives still mirror those of Biblical heroes—petty, short, envious, foolish, adulterous, filled with longing for a child, a home, meaning.

However, what's still delayed is the promised redemption of my youth, 2,000 years and counting. And the world suffers through digression after digression—a bombing in Nagasaki, The Peloponnesian War, the death of an unnamed child from malaria, a single butterfly flexing the variegated colors on its back in the garden—waiting forever.

As time passes, the weeks in which I'm writing and rewriting this essay, I find myself also working on an essay that I've written about trains: wedding trains, trains traveling through Europe, through the walls of limestone caves, the theoretical train that Einstein used to prove special relativity. I think the editing is almost done, but, like the comment from an old writing professor, like the point at the beginning of the universe, more compression is always possible. But I find compression difficult. The Bible, as I've detailed above, uses compression as a device to reduce the impact of our lives. And though I agree we are insignificant, like many other thinkers, I think that makes our brevity meaningful. This stance would seem to be contradictory, but I'd submit that much of our lives take place in contradiction, in the space between the spoken word and response.

Rather, like the universe now, I want expansion. I want to read an essay that carries within it all possibilities, all shades of meaning, all worlds of dinosaurs, of squid wandering on land, of Tony Allen making and missing layups, of me, leaving and unleaving my former wife, of the time I was a four at the ballet and laughed gleefully at the children spilling out from beneath a dancer's voluminous dress, of waterfalls spilling from mountaintops and dynasties crumbling, The Great Wall being erected and Trajan's column. Imagine an essay that went on longer than Proust, longer than Knausgaard, but that covered every train of thought, from Heraclitus and Euripides to the idle musings of a street sweeper in Paris, 1937, the passing thoughts of a young mother while her children play in the sprinkler in 1958. An essay that reimagines the brevity of human life as beautiful by capturing all of it, every blade of grass, every patch of daffodils.

Sadly, this is not that essay. This essay, unlike that dense point of compression, is unlikely to create space and time, gravity and the Milky Way. It is unlikely to create the elements, to set the stars burning and gas giants collecting dust; nor will it set the path of the moon, who's reflection lies silver on the ocean. Rather, this essay will merely move through space and time, like a train, like a sentence, like an emotion through a solitary Sunday morning of a man's mid-life malaise, alone, mid-winter, slate sky, the children now sleeping at their mother's a block away.

It is now Thursday morning. Time moves on like the obscenity that it is.

Once, a mad man shot the President from a hill. Once, the earth had two moons that smashed into each other and one was lost to the vast reaches of space. Once, a child, pink and peach colored, freshly unwombed, held my finger in her hand. Once, that same little girl read *Harry Potter* in her small bed, stopping at the scary parts, so I could sit with her as she read. Once, passenger pigeons flooded our sight as though they were ink spilled on pages of the sky. Once, I knelt in a tiny room full of roses and proposed to a woman. Once I lay with my son cradled in the hollow of my chest, warm in sleep. Once, I sat in artificial light, thinking all these thoughts—all the things I've left undone, as though finally, years removed from religion, I had become a proper Episcopalian.

All things are full of weariness, Ecclesiastes.

The Pacers now have a 32-22 lead on the New York Knicks. The game is still taking place in the present time. The score will not, barring some catastrophe—the universe ripping itself to shreds, Yellowstone erupting, a meteor hitting the Yucatan Peninsula—remain as 32-22 for an indefinite period of time. It is extremely unlikely, though not impossible, that neither team will score another basket.

I am doubled by the bathroom mirror. I notice, in the reflection of my life, the ghostly shape of a spider threading its way down from the ceiling. And now we are both doubled, looking, I'd imagine, not at one another, but at the reflections of ourselves, the reverse of the way we actually appear. It is a shame that I can only see this reflection and not see, instead, the reflection of myself in the eyes of my college roommate when I started dating the girl he had a crush on, or that of my mother this year, when I forgot to call on her birthday, that of my wife as we sat on the porch and I told her that we should part, that of my brother on the cross-country drive when I said that I hated him. I regret that I cannot show my neighbor, yelling just now, the reflection of his voice, hammering through the walls as he shouts at his daughter. I hope that no one ever writes about me or the shouting I've done at my recalcitrant daughter.

My face has grown weary of itself, or so it seems as I stare. Stare long enough and you'll be reminded of every psychological thriller, reminded of the way we are all slowly losing our minds.

Except my own life tends to be a bit boring: no spidey sense developing, no face that breaks into a cruel smile revealing a split personality, no aliens emerging from my stomach. No, just the cold and inexorable passage of time, making small outlines at the corner of my eyes, at the edges of my cheekbones, turning and turning the details of my life over like a leaf in a storm, furrowing brow and greying hairs at the temples.

I wipe the spider away with a Kleenex, this contingent arachnid taken quickly from the world. It is as though, for this brief blip of time, that I am not a contingent creature, who soon will be wiped clear from the mirror of time.

I try to explain to the spider, who can no longer listen, something of scale. I say the mere fact that I'm able to consider myself in the mirror, to muse over the Big Bang, the feeling of silk—soft as passing rain, the kiss I shared with Sasha in the dark in 1998, the dull ache of my shoulder as I carried the front left of my grandmother's coffin—reifies my decision to end his/her life. The development of consciousness, up here in the ragged world of skyscrapers, GDP and thrift savings plans, seems to entitle us to so much death dealt without awareness, without understanding, like a drone hovering over a gathering of strangers in the night.

The spider and I didn't cover much ground. Though perhaps it would have been for nothing anyway. Spiders are notoriously poor listeners, but renowned for their singing, which is lovely and soul-piercing but cannot be heard by human ears.

My lover and I sit in this city of trees beneath an awning shedding rain, amidst the smell of wet asphalt and petrichor. We are in a silent fight, which gives me space to be alone. I'm thinking about the children, how tender their feet once were. And about the solo trip I took to Spain—the way I found an orange tree behind a chain-link fence and photographed it, thinking the way the light was passing through the fence, illuminating the cracked earth and the dusty limbs of the tree, was somehow a work of art as much as the funhouse of Gaudi's Parc Guell. There are so many moments I still need to share—that time I was seven and skipped stones on the back of Lindo Channel, that time I sat at my first night in college in Santa Barbara, 800 miles from home, talking to Iris about all the things I'd wanted to say in high school within the velvet folds of night, that night I sat among the Eucalyptus and listened to the wind mimicking the ocean, feeling as though my whole life would be full of wonder.

You see, my lovely reader, I say, as we lean in together, I would like this essay to be about time. And since I can't expand it to include everything I'd like to, I see now that the best mode is compression. I'd like to compress all these moments down into a single paragraph, a single sentence, a single word, a single letter. I'd like to tell you what I've been thinking about these past few months that we've been apart, that we've been together, that have passed since I wasn't your child anymore, wasn't your lover, your neighbor, your husband, your friend, the many things I've wanted to tell you from 3,000 miles away, from across the city, from exactly where you are, without having to say anything at all. I want the quiet compression of things before there was any space, before there was any time, only these billions and billions of moments, unborn.

Departures

The world cares little for our departures. It spins and spins in the dark unaware that we are even here, spinning in that same dark. We are left to construct our own signs then, spin our own yarns about the moments that have marked us. We tell ourselves stories about first loves, parents, home, in order to give our lives structure, a foundation on which to build the architecture of the self. The meaning of our departures comes in hindsight, a postscript. Leaving is not the car going down the driveway, the hand waving goodbye; it is considering, days, months, years later, what the leaving meant, trying to remember if you held your hand against the cold glass and what it meant that your mother didn't cry. This essay is already a failure, an attempt to send myself a postcard from the future. I doubt I'll have the sense to read it.

The last summer I spent in Chico, CA before leaving home was like any other: blazingly, soul-scorchingly, hot. It was the sort of heat about which people out east say, "It's a dry heat though," which is why I dislike almost everyone out east. The observation is made no less obnoxious by its veracity. The summer days in Washington, D.C. are sauna-like, something to be endured, like watching golf on television. These relentless days always leave me longing for the cool California nights of my youth—crickets chirping and a light breeze prickling night's skin.

Departing for college was the first of many adult severances. It felt like a pinprick at the time, an inevitable retracing of the steps taken by siblings and friends. They returned in the summers, strangers in a familiar land, stopping for a visit with the natives before returning to their new home. And yet, as the years have passed and college friendships and memories have faded, I realize that leaving Chico was a severance, an end to the era of a childhood and a farewell to my home, and to the idea of any place being home.

It's difficult to be nostalgic for something you haven't yet left. It's now that I remember our sloped driveway—basketball hoop nailed into the roof—countless afternoons spent shooting as the sun faded behind purpling cathedrals of clouds. It's now that I miss the tangled oaks, with knots like the hands of grandmothers that line the streets of downtown, now that I miss the dappled light flickering across the water of Lindo Channel. Perhaps what I mean to say when I say I miss home is that I miss childhood, that I ache for innocence—card games, stick wars, picking plump blackberries from the ground, the succulent sweetness of them midsummer. And then it's gone, in a flash, and I am older again, peering back as it nears midnight.

I spent that final summer before college scraping aged wallpaper from the cornices and lees of a sunroom in a quiet house of clapboard siding and shutters, converted twenty years prior from an old farmhouse. I was doing the work for a member of our church, John. John was an older man, with a quick smile and a head wreathed in white hair that made him the envy of any good Franciscan. Our chats about the work and how it was to be done were brief, which was good because I wasn't good at the work.

I don't know that I've ever been "good" at anything. That is not entirely true. I believe I was good at the multiplication tables, near great. But no one ever made a statue for knowing quickly that six times six is thirty-six. I should say that work didn't suit me, and that I didn't suit the work, and that no work ever suits me except that which I have chosen, and, even then, after a while, it no longer suits me, or I get bored and restless and feel unsuited for work.

What I remember most vividly is John's daughter, Jen. She was a year younger than I was, and I'd carried a torch for her since we were children, or maybe I only carried a torch for her that summer, or perhaps, even now, I am only remembering that I carried a torch for her that summer before I left for college, when in fact, I only carried a real torch for her when we were children, or maybe I never carried a torch for her at all.

My desire for Jen was not complex. My desire for Jen was randomly generated. She had the good fortune of being of the female sex, which meant that I desired her. This is not a Shakespearean romance. It is the unique traits of the beloved, dimples, skin color, hairstyle, and length, slight overbite, slender legs, etc. that set them apart from the masses, move them from abstraction to reified whole. She had black hair, I remember that much, though it might have been dyed blond, or it was blond and had been dyed black. Or maybe it was red but had been dyed blond and black at different times of the summer. I remember that it was short, of that I can be certain, I think.

I was an untutored youth, not familiar with semiotic theory, and so I believed my attraction for specific women was unique to the collection of molecules and atoms that comprised my being. I didn't even know the word trope and thus, did not know that loving itself was a trope, though later in life, I was to discover the word trope and reapply it to periods of time in my life, wondering if I'd known the word then I'd have identified them as tropes, or whether you would only apply the word to a portion of your life in the past tense because to imply that a moment in your life is a trope as it's happening is to take all the fun out of existing, to make it less mercurial than determinate.

Perhaps I never should have learned the word trope.

I labored that summer in the pre-iPod era, an era that included a shocking amount of silence. What does one do with brute silence? Plays games, I suppose, constructs poems or melodies about the particular play of light on the wall or the nuthatches song melodically slipping through the limbs of old elms. I did none of these things. I have to be writing to be thinking. My mind, if given silence and time, plays a cruel and useless game. It spins in circles like a top. I think I thought of two things, just how damn hard it was to scrape paint from a wall, and whether or not Jen found me attractive. The paint was hard to scrape from the walls, and Jen did find me attractive, I think, or she found me passable, or attractive but unapproachable. I never got around to asking her.

Her voice from a far-off room would set off a series of intense physical reactions, increased heart rate, pinpricks on the scalp and neck, along with elaborate fantasies involving hay, period costuming, and a good deal of sweat. As in all romantic relationships carried out exclusively in the mind, when we actually spoke it was shot through with cold doses of reality. The beloved is partly the beloved because she is nothing at all. She's a shadow on the wall of Plato's Cave, a puppet constructed and controlled by the strings of another's mind.

In truth, I was hoping to write an essay about love and home, or women and home, or sex and leaving. And yet, I find myself fumbling to write about any of them. Home is a collection of ideas rather than a place, women: an abstraction, sex: a distraction. Perhaps what I am writing about is merely a summer, a bit of ephemera dredged up to be looked over like a pan for gold.

They say that the DNA of a child gets locked into the birthing mother's body. The same is true of the women I have loved, the places I have called home. They are a part of me, even now, when I am so distant from them.

You see, leaving the safe haven of my hometown, of my baseball cards and fantasy novels, was also to leave behind imagined love: the sort where you could carry a torch for someone without ever speaking to them, the sort where walking past them after class, even if they didn't smile at you, the mere fact of occupying space in their vicinity was enough to leave you floating away in a manner that would have pleased Peter Pan. I quickly moved from the general to the specific in college. Women were no longer phantoms and succubeses, but corporeal beings with artsy dispositions possessed of idle chatter, or beautiful and unattainable girls with boyfriends in distant cities. To love generally, non-specifically, as I did before I left home, was safe. The heartaches engendered by phantoms are frequent but less seismic.

In truth, it is a challenge for all romantics to have the fine texture, woven from silken dreams, made into crude and disappointing flesh. Life, for any good romantic, is better observed, better dreamed, better imagined than actually lived. The basic failure of the romantic temperament is that it is more pleasurable to sit across the room and peer at one's lover than to sit with her and discuss the weather or day's events. She might tell you that it was sunny in the afternoon, and you might add that it was a bit breezy, and this will be your evening. She might tell you about her brother when you really wanted to hear about her sister, or she might need to blow her nose when you wanted her to kiss you. It's just these sorts of inconveniences that make loving a person so unwieldy.

Knowing now the fallacy of romantic love, I understand that a person generates fantasies about home and about being a child as well. A home is less an authentic space moored in a place and time than an idea. It's a series of memories burnished by the years into something golden.

The strawberries in the side yard of my neighbor's house were not just strawberries, but the best strawberries I'd ever eaten. The dappled light in Bidwell Park is not just the dappled light of any park, but the finest dappling of light that I've ever seen in my life. You would want to dapple everything in this light, trust me. These false constructions are what makes being a human being livable. Imagine if our insignificance was routinely made manifest?

Home is the place where I peed in the backyard. Home is the place where I gathered dandelions. Home is the place where I threw a blanket over a heater and trapped in the warmth. Home is the place where I was loved very deeply and specifically, as it seems to me now, only a child can be loved.

Perhaps I'm just trying to force meaning, for we are animals of meaning, onto a summer devoid of it. Perhaps that summer meant nothing. And yet, I remember deconstructing a deck, pausing on the iridescent glimmer of a snake's shed skin. And later, after we had finished pulling out the rotten boards, we rebuilt the deck, putting new boards over that shed skin, burying it yet again. For the purposes of the metaphor, imagine that the skin did not move, imagine that I am a skin, imagine that a summer and a self are like skin, easy to shed.

Her name back then was different. It was near Easter. Her cheeks were pale and round. She was wearing a blue dress with white polka dots. We were sitting on the crushed grass in her parent's back yard, counting the small chocolate candies gathered from plastic eggs. And then, just like that, it's gone, and the next thing I remember is five kids, her included, wandering onto the train tracks that ran behind her house, though our parents had promised that there would be hell to pay if we did. I remember the older kids talking about putting a penny on the tracks, talking about how that might derail the train. And then, the small breeze of a late April day, thin clouds making whorls as if they are fingertips. We are waiting for the train. Oh please let it come before our parents arrive and carry us home.

[after Montaigne]

On Trains

CHILDHOOD

Our parents constantly reminded us to stay away from the tracks. Parents are always nattering on about things to avoid—eating before exercise, eating before bed, eating in bed, crossing the street without looking both ways, acquiring a lover who is ten years older with an addiction to Xanax, not getting grossly drunk at a wedding and peeing in the azaleas—that it eventually becomes hard to imagine they had any fun in their own probably non-existent childhoods. It's tempting to imagine them eating gruel after putting in eight hours at the factory or scrubbing dishes in the afternoon and copying out their names in perfect cursive before falling asleep at seven. And thus, as any child knows, adults are always to be feared, but not always to be trusted. To trust them would be to accept the adult world, which every child knows is full of seriousness and obligations that have very little to do with joy.

Naturally, whatever a parent forbids becomes alluring. We could not fully conceive what was so dangerous about the tracks. We were children, not stupid. We understood you did not stand directly in front of the train for fun. And yet we knew some further danger lurked beneath the surface because it was forbidden to us. And so, this journey, though it only spanned a couple of blocks, was a childhood passage of rites. We understood that we were not traveling through a hole in a fence into waist-high patches of grass to stand near the tracks that cut like a black scar behind those suburban fences. We knew instead we were traveling from the safe land of mother's skirts, of milk and cookies and bedtimes into a foreign and dangerous land. And parts of ourselves we didn't know existed wanted to court danger. Parts we'd rediscover later in life, chasing strange lovers, girls with gaps in their teeth who smoked unfiltered cigarettes, where we'd watch them against a blue horizon, blowing smoke into that same blue. We'd stare at these women for hours, losing ourselves in them, when all we'd intended to do was pass time reading about epistemology.

We were out by the tracks to see if the train would flatten a penny. We'd seen these pennies before, cupped in the palms of adults or more fortunate children. We were determined to make that particular day the one of our own becoming, a day we'd share with less fortunate children in our own unknowable futures.

We often pass childhood off as a fairy tale, thinking of the fun and games. And yet, my childhood, like many others, was more like something from the Brothers Grimm, enchanted and dangerous both. There was a possibility the train would derail, or that we, through some act of stupidity or bravery, would wind up on the tracks. We did not know then that all of life was to be like that afternoon, that the mere act of existence is a risk—driving on a freeway, waking in the morning, taking the late train home, talking with a stranger deep into the night.

I'll never forget the enchantment and fear of that day. We ached for arrival and absence, yearning for the train's whistle and fearing it, wanting our parents to remain away forever, so we could experience something for once, and wanting them to gather us in their arms, tousle our hair, and assure us we would always be safe.

What if things had gone on a different track? What if the train had come earlier? Or we'd decided to throw rocks at it? Or placed the penny down at the wrong moment? Perhaps a universe exists where the train did come, where the solid black cars flattened the grass and slid over a penny. Perhaps a universe exists where the train never came at all, where we stood with muddy shoes waiting in silence for something absent, like love affairs with women whose faces are now gone to us. Perhaps a universe exists where I stepped out onto the tracks and discovered the mystery. In that universe, the train exists, but I, and this piece of writing, and therefore you, no longer exist. Instead, we are riding along together into another place.

A WEDDING

She wore white that day, as is the contemporary custom. Apparently, we've Queen Victoria to thank for the tradition. We're also to thank her for the presence of bridesmaids to carry the train. And, it becomes quickly apparent why the woman had an entire era of western literature named in her honor. She's commandeered at least two major elements of the most momentous day in people's lives, or at least the day with the most riding on it. Samuel Johnson said of his friend Thomas Carlyle, "It was a blessing he and his wife Jane married one another: thereby making only two people unhappy, rather than four."

My wife wore a semi-cathedral length train. I can only discern that from the pictures. The memories of my wedding day are scattered, like the page of a magazine that's been put through a shredder.

I'm not usually one to balk at tradition. I married a woman who wore white, drank moderately, and celebrated Christmas with a tree and Midnight Mass. And yet, it seems to me that the tradition of carrying the wedding train into the church was a false step, an apt metaphor lost. Marriage is a mixture of the sacred and the profane. The train, dragged along the floor, gathering bits of grime on its route is symbolic of what's to come. A person can call another his love and still almost hate her on certain afternoons. Marriage is not clean.

Here is my ideal wedding: I'd like to see an argument over whether divorced parents are sitting far enough away. I'd like to see the bride and groom argue over how much they're paying the band followed by a conversation about contributions to a 403b. I'd like to see a first dance where the groom breakdances and the bride waltzes around him in perfect timing. In short, I'd like to see people begin that damned honorable and difficult pastime of being married for all of us to see. And let the train's dirty hem be the first sign.

I could not grab onto anything that sunny August morning, nine years past when I made the most important decision of my life. It was as if my younger self was somehow aware the fabric of his reality was about to shredded, and so he wanted to observe the whole thing from afar, as if to say, so this is getting married, I wonder how that fool down there will feel in the morning.

Perhaps the day is better described in this way: It was like boarding a train in the middle of the night, finding oneself a comfortable seat straight away and leaning against the cool window, falling into a deep slumber. And then slithering through the night, passing through cities with names you don't know, passing by the darkened windows of cathedrals from another era and arriving at the end of the line, awakened by a shake on the shoulder, quickly wiping the drool from the window, hoping only you were privy to the indignity of existence before stepping out into the caesious morning light, trying to make sense of this new city, with gables on all the doorways, and serpentine streets with peculiar names and all the women walking quickly in large straw hats. Here I am, you say, and begin walking across the cobbles.

ON EUROPE

We took the train from Bologna to Venice. Either I hadn't been on a train in years, or I'd never been on a train. It's disgraceful how as one ages it becomes hard to corroborate memories with reality. And, this being my first ride, everything appeared as new—hillsides dusted in houses, skeins of sunlight filtering through tall grass that lined arterials madcapping their way through the countryside. The clothes strung across lines were not just clothes strung across lines; they were Italian clothes strung across Italian lines.

It is precisely that unfamiliarity, which wakes us in travel, making it a joy akin to romance. Travel provides the fiction of being someone else. No trip has been ruined with more rapidity than by the reminder you are still traveling as yourself: irritable most mornings, slightly vain, given to laziness, and cursed with stale opinions you've not cultivated but stolen from whatever magazine you'd read that week. Being oneself can spoil all the novelty in the world.

The trouble with trains is they are too slow. I'd pay any amount to be able to travel fast enough to leave behind this sad husk of a self that I've cobbled together over the past three decades. I wonder what speeds would have to be reached to turn this collection of molecules into something more useful?

I remember the skeletal outline of ships as we approached the station, sails stowed, lines cutting through the sky, and the narrow strip of rail, like an exposed vertebrae guiding us in to the brain stem of Venice. This is precisely why a person rides on a train: to see the countryside in a different way—no distractions of crying children, speed limit signs, quick on and offs, or a wife who keeps telling you it's not okay to look at the sunset rather than the road, which ends with an argument about aesthetics and ephemerality.

The question is whether the countryside is always romantic, and we just don't take the time to see it, or if the countryside is rarely romantic and it is only the train or the vacation that makes it so, i.e., are we merely creatures of perception who live by illusion?

I'd like to believe the train has some magic, but I'd be a fool. Whether it's the ships in Venice or the backlot of a McDonald's in Cleveland, what we see is one microscopic bit of an entirely unimaginable whole, and our small bit has been colored by our upbringing, our parents, our ethnicity, our mood, how stiff our coffee was that morning. We're contingent creatures viewing the world through kaleidoscopes. The only rational proposal is that we all continually board trains to cities we've never been in so we might occasionally escape ourselves.

When trains first arrived people were decrying their use as degradation when compared with the quality of the world as seen from the top of the coach. Society is never short on curmudgeons or people who see the past as idyllic and the present as rubbish. The present is rubbish, but we've not the time for that. What has changed with each new mode of transport, and I'll grant the curmudgeons this, is our relation to the world around us. It changes our perception to pass over a city, five miles above, as opposed to traveling through it at five miles an hour. In this way, Kansas City becomes a string of lights, and though one can imagine the thousands of lives there, it is only in the abstract, for a few minutes before the lights fade into darkness. But you see, these trains of thought are only loosely connected, and it takes only a slight detour to end up in a new car.

ON THE POSSIBILITY OF MAKING LOVE WITH A FRENCH WOMAN ON A TRAIN

Make your way into the dining car. Ask the woman with the golden hair who is staring out the window if there is room for one more: order caviar and toast. Tell her you are American. Take your time looking out the window. Mention the countryside and the clouds. Have a glass of wine. One is enough. Ask after her children. Tell her about your grandmother's farm. If you do not have a grandmother, feel free to embellish. Meet her eyes every ten seconds or so, hold her glance for a millisecond, then blush.

When you are touching the leg of a French woman on a train begin with the pointer finger on your left hand. Place it just above the knee of her left leg, extending your middle finger to join it. Move your two fingers in small circles, moving further up her leg with each passing comment. Maintain eye contact throughout. Do not look away. This may be your one chance to make love to a French woman on a train. When she asks if you'd like another glass, look deeply into her eyes to determine the answer. Look away without answering. Comment on the simple beauty of the countryside, how it reminds you of time passing, the small intervals of lives you see beyond the window, how it reminds you of all the things you haven't done. Say, "I need to get something from my sleeper car."

As you rise, use the index finger on your right hand and slide it across the palm of her left hand. Begin just below the base of the middle finger, and slide it down the center of her hand, finishing at the base just where the thumb joint begins. As your finger reaches the base of her hand, retrace your steps by sliding it gently upwards at a forty-five-degree angle. The fingers should be touching for no more than two seconds. It is important that you slide the finger up, not continuing onto her wrist. During the time your finger is sliding down the length of her palm, raise the left side of your mouth slightly, something just beneath a smile, and hold her eyes. Take three steps before turning around to look over your left shoulder, if she meets your eyes, raise your right hand to your face as though you are scratching it. Use your index finger to point in her direction, followed by your three middle fingers pulled slightly back toward your face, though without touching it, to indicate she should follow you. If the woman is looking down or away when you turn over your left shoulder, keep walking: It is not your day to make love to a French woman on a train.

And as you pee in the bathroom and straighten your hair in the mirror before returning to your own seat, notice today has turned out like any other day in your life, and like the many that are sure to follow, an infinite seeming number of days in which you have not made love to a French woman, and certainly not on a train.

ON RELATIVITY

Einstein used trains, well, passengers on those trains to help elucidate his theory of special relativity. Imagine two people; make them attractive if it helps keep your attention. The first, a woman, mid-thirties, black shoulder-length hair, recently cut, is sitting on a car near the front of the train. She is paring her fingernails, reading Henry James and wondering if she will be picked up by her husband at the station. There is a slight chance he will not be there. Before she'd left, they'd had a fight over credit cards, though something deeper was underlying it all. Secretly, she knew they were both happy she was leaving. And yet, after a weekend away, sitting in conference rooms listening to speakers drone on about coming changes in fonts, watching flies bump frantically into screens, or the tinted water slapping the wooden boats gently in the harbor; she missed him.

The second person, Jon, is standing on the platform watching the train pass. He watches the train pass, ticketless, feeling a sense of stasis. He watches it knowing he cannot leave, but something must change. He knows if he left, nothing would change. And so he watches the train, thinking about what it might be like to change. The cars slide through the space that was previously empty. Most days, after they pass, he stares out onto a field of clover, limitless green sky.

As the train approaches the platform, it is struck by two bolts of lightning: one of the bolts strikes the front of the train, the other strikes the back. Jon concludes that the two bolts occurred at the same time. He also concludes time is nebulous, a figment of his imagination, and there will always be time for change. He doesn't stand by the tracks again for years.

The woman on the train, because she is moving toward the strike at the front of the train, perceives that lightning struck the train on the front first. And the bolt that struck the train in back happened milliseconds later. Who is correct?

They both are. Two people can perceive the same event in different ways; the synchronicity of our lives is an illusion. Perhaps that is why you look at me with horror when I tell you I could live forever, watching everyone around me die, and taking pleasure in the persistence of life. And you perceive me as some sort of monster, and you, I perceive as a liar.

ON CONNECTION

A train is a series of rails, hammered together one tie at a time. You can see how art might turn a train into a metaphor. It is a metaphor for marriage, the ties that bind us together. It is a metaphor for the passage of time. It is a metaphor for man's need for connection and domination. A train can be a part of a dress, a digression, a means of proving Newton was wrong. A train can be any of these things. It can even be a place where we meet.

ON YOU AND I

I think of you when I think of trains, of your purple fingernails tapping the window and the tip of your tongue worrying the inside of your left cheek. The countryside is slipping past—cows, heather, bails of golden hay, celadon skies, trees shaped like the backs of bent pilgrims, everything present to itself—as we glide over the rails. I locked eyes with you before I sat and pulled a book from my bag, something by Mann I couldn't focus on because I had already been caught in the thick headlights of your gaze.

And now we are sitting here, as time too—a bang, a meteor in the Yucatan, shale, the death of an archduke, certain cloud shapes against a dark horizon from evenings we've lived before, listening to the sound of distant rain—passes us by, in a courtly dance. And I keep telling myself after this chapter, this paragraph, this sentence, this word I'll put the book down, I'll stop writing this essay, and ask your name. Your name could be anything. The moment is always passing.

Years from now, we'll tell the story to a disinterested couple over a bottle of port, how we met on a train traveling to the South of France. We'll leave out the part about my handshaking, the weak coffee, the waiter's pencil-thin mustache, a chip in the side of your cup because we'll have forgotten them beneath the avalanche of days. We'll lie awake at night after the visiting couple leaves, dissecting the evening like a cadaver, reflecting on how strange it was that we were once nameless to each other, these two people who are now so tired of one another's hair, skin, eyebrows and harmless jokes. We'll lie in our bed and wish our bodies belonged to strangers waiting in some distant city for a connection to bring them home.

On Eating Animals

As I've aged, I find I've changed in certain ways that extend beyond the physical manifestations of ear hair and crow's feet, which are attendant parts of my thirties. One of these changes is a newfound attentiveness to food. I grew up in a single-parent home where a weekend delicacy was getting tuna fish sandwiches with Kraft singles melted on them. Thus, discovering gustatory pleasure as one of life's pleasures has been a surprise. When I travel now, I scour the internet for days in advance, opening menus and mapping out the location of the best new eats in a city—hot chicken, slow-smoked brisket, foie gras, creperies with grape arbors, vines casting lattices of shade over tables of wrought iron. I scroll through lists of best of's—an action a previous iteration of myself would have sneered at—best beer garden, best rooftop bar, best farm to table restaurant, best happy hour, best cheese dipped in other artisanal cheese. This love of food doesn't make me a unique specimen of the human race. After all, human beings have been harvesting crops and hunting animals since we climbed down from trees in the Great Rift Valley.

My desire for good food has led me into the literature about food at a time when it lies at the center of our cultural zeitgeist. Though what I mean by cultural zeitgeist is middle-class interest. Food has become a catch-all for our insatiable desire to be entertained: cooking shows, shows about baking cupcakes, shows about baking cakes, shows about the running of kitchens, the running of restaurants, Instagram as the site of food porn, writing about food, about chefs, about farmer's markets, about farm to table, food as the locus of meaning in neighborhoods and cultures. I'm not, let me just be honest here, incisive enough to tackle the exclusionary class politics behind *The Omnivore's Dilemma* or the problematic socioeconomic demographics that no doubt influenced the arterial line of Whole Foods opening along a stretch of Wisconsin Avenue in upscale Washington, D.C., eliding the poorer neighborhoods that branch off across Rock Creek Park. Rather, I'm going to focus on the narrow subgenre of the food essay. This is where, as a sometimes writer, and voracious reader, I make my way in the world and find my locus of meaning.

The food essay is, mind you, unlike my newfound love of food which includes numerous dipping sauces for French fries—garlic mayo, chipotle mayo, mayo mayo—not about food. The literary food essay is invariably about family. As Tolstoy said, every happy family eats food, but every unhappy family eats food in a way that can reveal fractured associations related to childhood drama. It's pithier in the original Russian. As such, every food essay veers quickly from the proper way to brown butter just so into a piece of writing that reveals a complicated relationship with the essayist's mother, or a connection to a grandmother's Scandinavian heritage via an old cookie recipe on an index card. Recipe cards and recipes, in general, are gold for an essayist, giving structure to an essay and therefore a form to our memories and lives, which have no definite shape but float on like water, like yeast in dough, subterranean, dark.

What I'm really whining about is that I feel excluded from crafting a good food essay. My single-parent home, full of fish sticks, hot cheese sandwiches and trips to McDonald's, has no resolution around braised pork shoulder, no moment where flour settled on the rolling pin as light filtered in a warped glass window. I cannot see my grandmother's weathered hands lovingly shaping the dough as her wind chimes swing leisurely together on a sun-filled northern California afternoon. Or perhaps I can see exactly that, but I'm resistant, like every good contrarian to spinning that same yarn, the smell of salami and apple juice as I walked into my grandmother's house, reminding me of her Italian heritage. I don't want to read those treacly stories and have food illuminate family. I want to read something that cuts closer, where the marbles of fat and ridges of bone are clean and clear.

Though it's just as likely that I don't like food essays because my love of food has arrived later in life and everyone else has already discovered and written about food in ways that I can't even approach.

Although, if I left off all of life's activities because someone else had already gotten there and done it better, I wouldn't drive a car, I never would have ridden a horse, crafted a sentence, and I'd be a virgin. But I digress, as I often do, though often it's merely to tell a pun and then point out to the already bored audience the intricacies of why calling the kids a turkey while they prepared turkey was such a verbal coup. In another version of this essay, rather than complaining about the exclusionary politics of the food essay, I'd write something full of puns on the words trifle and filling until the reader was stuffed, but I haven't written it yet. At the end of an argument, it's best to demonstrate your proof. Thus, I'll employ an old axiom I picked up in graduate school creative writing workshops: show, don't tell.

HOW TO ROAST A DOG

Do not befriend the dog. This will complicate your relationship. If he looks at you with longing in his deep brown eyes, it is best to turn away. Do not name the dog. Do not let your children name the dog. Do not let anyone play a game of fetch or tug of war with the dog. Do not let anyone pet the dog, or express to you in any sort of way that they feel a kinship with the creature.

If you must give him a name, call him dog. Dogs are crafty. He may whine in the backyard, or attempt to bring you a tennis ball. Do not, under any circumstances, take the tennis ball from his mouth or mime a throwing motion. If you feel tempted, remind yourself that if you do not eat this dog, you will spend the rest of your life cleaning up his shit and taking him on walks. Consider how few of the things in your life have turned out as you wanted—jobs, wives, mothers, sons, certain family trips—and ask yourself if you want to add cleaning shit and 5am walks to that list.

Tether him to something sturdy in the yard. If he runs around and barks, remind yourself that that is just the sort of annoying thing that gets you eaten. Do not direct your conversation at the dog. He will take this as encouragement and wag his tail. A wagging tail is precisely the sort of thing that you want to avoid.

People are going to judge you for eating your dog. Be prepared. Do not allow these neighbors and friends to gain the upper hand. Explain to them that in a variety of cultures it is considered silly to tame dogs, to not periodically roast them over an open spit. If they point out that you are not living in that culture say that we are living in a unified world of personhood. Use personhood. Say it meaningfully. Imply that they would have said something sexist like the brotherhood of man.

If your know-it-all neighbor, the one who is always out jogging early in the morning with the dog at his side, making everyone else feel bad for wanting to sleep in one goddamn day, tells you that a dog is man's best friend, correct him. Let him know that the status of dog as man's best friend is indicative of the denuded state of human relationships. Tell him that man's best friend is God if the neighbor is religious. If he's been seeing a psychoanalyst, remind him that his best friend is himself, the only person he can count on. Mention self-care or the virtue of hard work. Remind your other liberal neighbor who is not seeing a psychoanalyst that the rise of canines as a surrogate family member is really a sign of the degradation of the modern familial unit, and worse, absolution of the civic responsibility to his fellow man.

If the dog persists in fetching tennis balls from the children, bringing your slippers and being willing to go for walks after 8am, name him "Old Yeller." Explain to the neighbors that he is rabid and that you've seen him eyeing their children meaningfully, and if they say that all they've seen is tail-wagging, say that it's a sign of aggression in that particular breed of dog.

Imply that you practically invented the breed.

The dog should be cooked for no more than an hour on an open spit. Remove the skin first. If you've a gas grill, it's best to cut him up into steaks. It turns out that dog is meat like any other. Before you take a bite of him, pray to God, or the Gaia spirit or Allah and thank them for bringing food into the world. You have not done a terrible thing. You have just done a thing amongst many other things.

HOW TO FRY A SQUIRREL

You'll need to buy a weapon that shoots small bullets. You don't want to fill a squirrel with too much lead or you'll ruin the flavor. This is not the Wild West, and you are not the Lone Ranger or John Wayne. You are a sad and strange person who is hunting squirrels in her suburban neighborhood. If you've got a choice between grey and black squirrels, start with the grey ones as they have more meat on them.

The trick to getting a squirrel is that you need to keep very still. At first, get them accustomed to having the window open. Stand near the window, whistle to pass the time, waving to this or that squirrel as if they are uncles and cousins standing across the room at a family reunion. Eventually, you can open the door and move onto a bench in the middle of the yard.

Imagine that you are the Saint Francis of Assisi. Feel the flow of the world, the goodness of everything around you, the particular tenor of dappled light coming through the oak tree, the sweet smell of the honeysuckle and the Black-eyed Susan's taking over everything in the yard. Do not actually become Saint Francis of Assisi or you will never eat a squirrel. If you become Saint Francis of Assisi, you will feel a oneness with the world, with the crickets chirping in the grass, the violets swaying in the breeze, and you will forget the cold world that runs just beneath this one where once someone pushed you in line and yelled into your face, shouting that you were a piece of shit, which, deep down, you felt to be true. Remain areligious for this activity.

Squirrels are best eaten alone. Eating a squirrel, like many things in life, is another opportunity for honoring the self. Gently salt and pepper the squirrel, adding a touch of lime. Pour yourself a glass or three of table wine. The squirrel is unlikely to taste particularly good or bad. Ignore the taste, focus on the world around you, which you have been so disconnected from in this last unhappy stretch of things with your seasonal depression kicking in, your boss reminding you of small mistakes, being alone this fall again, thinking of your mother's sadness, and all the goddamn inequality and silliness of this country. Think instead of the things that make you feel whole—friendship, laughter, adventure, the look of a fat bee buzzing around the garden come spring, his legs gently alighting on the bloom of a flower. As you set down your utensils, clattering on the plate, think of nothing other than what is happening, the play of light on the slats of the fence, the wind rustling the leaves of the oak, the day passing into the blue of an early evening.

ON EATING YOUR SPOUSE

This is not the sort of thing that one plans for. To have and to hold, to watch summer rainstorms swimming down from the sky, or babies, fat babies, poking their delighted little fingers into the air. "Look, she's smiling." But sometimes things go sideways. You may find yourself eating a pasta dish on a yellow plate that you've had for fifteen years, and you may ask yourself if the meaning of your life is to eat pasta dishes and watch Jeopardy on DVR to see if you could ever be a contestant on the show, but not really ever trying to get on the show, not filling out the paperwork or finding out what you'd have to do, like show up in Newark on a Saturday, not even knowing the smallest thing about how you might make your dream of being on Jeopardy come true, which, come to think of it, really isn't a dream but just something you've been telling yourself for a while, so that what had once seemed like a dream turned out to have been just a thing repeated enough times to take on the quality of the dream, when really, you just liked to DVR things. Is this all that life is about?

And you realize, as you think about the variety of things you haven't done or places you haven't been, that something needs to change, and so, after helping your wife to wash the dishes, careful to make sure all debris is removed to achieve the maximum amount of life and time from your dishwasher, without even asking what the point is of a dishwasher that requires you to pre-wash the dishes until they are immaculate because that's not the sort of rabbit hole that you want to fall down. On this particular evening, you crack open a bottle of red wine and suggest that you could rub your spouse's feet, and as you tenderly knead the heel of her foot with your fingers, you might tell her about a dream you had when you were younger, that came to you after reading books about explorers.

The phrase is until death do us part. Well, what better way to do the parting? Your spouse may not want to be eaten, and, truth be told, you may not want to eat your spouse. However, spouses are best with a bit of turmeric. Regardless of the outcome, this is an important fact to remember.

HUNTING COWS

I've always found it's best to rise early when hunting cows. Surely, it's easy to object to such a practice, cows are not notoriously difficult animals to corner. However, when you go out hunting for cows it is an entirely different thing than watching them through the shrouds of morning haze; what you are experiencing instead is an encounter, a joining of spirits. Besides which, it's a nice opportunity to try out that new recipe for Bloody Marys that you've had tucked away.

It's best to have company on these expeditions, preferably a person with a sense of humor. The sort of person who could laugh death in the face or at least get him to chuckle. The reason that this sort of humor is indispensable is that you're involved in an ugly business. Most of life is comprised of ugly things as you've no doubt gathered from your taxes, traffic jams, computer failures, and indignities too numerous to count.

It's inevitably cold on these mornings, and it's best to spend the first few minutes talking about just that to get it out of the way. Nothing ruins a good hunting trip like endless talk about the weather. The best part about hunting for cows is the conversation that takes place around the kitchen table after the talk of weather has subsided and before you leave. You might say, "What is the nature of reality or our place in it that we are able to contemplate the very cosmos that we are a part of?"

And your hunting partner might answer, "Have you considered the fact that every cosmos ever created, which might just be this one, you'd have to admit, is comprised of beings that contemplate their own existence? In essence, why do we assume that this is abnormal?"

Or you might tell your hunting partner that you are leaving your wife. "It's nothing in particular. Not a specific thing, per se. Rather, it's a whole collection of things, dishes, trash, sex, or lack thereof, kids, diapers, the trail of a comet across the sky that is now burned out, the way the bare trees look against an early setting sun."

And your partner might say, "Have you considered that your plight is not specific? That your unhappiness is not actually about you, but more a general statement about the poverty of relationships in the world." Your hunting partner might be this vaguely contemplative and argumentative type. You'd have to admit that this is precisely the sort of person you'd get stuck with.

All afternoon, the two of you watch the cows munching in the grass through slats in the fence. For some reason, you've left your guns inside and all you can do is stare at their broad backs, at the black and white splotches on their skin. In the silence, you hear house wrens and sparrows calling from the trees.

The cows have all gone back to the barn now. The moon is a hangnail now in some piece of the visible sky. The opportunity of a lifetime has been missed. But lifetime, at least it seems to you, is mostly about the opportunities that you don't take, the trips you weren't on, the random collection of atoms that is you that has seen but a small portion of this infinitely large universe, but a fraction even of the people who inhabit the earth at the moment you do. And so you do not lie down to sleep as sad as you did the night before, cold, alone, dreaming of the women you used to know. Tonight, you are happy, or something like it, having spent the day talking with an old friend about what it means to be human. Perhaps that's all there is or ever will be.

On Uncertainty

Briefly, I lived in uncertainty with a woman I loved. Although perhaps briefly is the wrong term to describe those years. In the relative span of a human life, years are not brief. Even if humans are but brevities on the long wave of time. This is not news though, and I fear the near erotic delight I take in digression has already led me astray. Let me begin again.

For a time then, while I was in love, I lived in a state of uncertainty. The entanglement being romantic, the uncertainty was particularly knotty, a row of bracken. We all live through uncertainties, between job offers, between colleges, between cities or suburbs, between political candidates, between varieties of apples. Indeterminacy is at the heart of any human life. But romantic indeterminacy provides the richest loam for sifting.

*

According to a 2016 study in *Nature Communications,* the stress of uncertain pain is greater than that of certain pain. Anyone who has waited for corporal punishment as a child knows the truth of this study, the fear that grips the mind at the thought of a smack across the bottom, which doubled and even tripled as you lay awaiting your punishment, and in my child mind, I'd think my father was going to wallop me so hard on my ass that I'd fly to the moon. Break-ups can be like that, haunting you long before you've come to the actual thing, and the pain takes on near mythic proportions, a ship's mast, a large head snaking above the water, a human-like form lumbering in the distance between the trees.

*

She and I knew that we wouldn't last. In those early days, we often talked about breaking it off, the necessity of parting ways, imagining how we'd reflect back on the intelligence of our decision, knowing we should part. We swore we'd remember our brief time together. Except, we didn't break it off. We remained. We persisted. So, our time together spun in the direction it was always going to. The Titanic didn't turn around. Manatees didn't turn into mermaids. The Loch Ness Monster was never found. This iteration of life was cast in marble, so that I can turn it around now, view it through new prisms.

Were we happy then, in the early days together? It's hard to remember, in part because our memories are as light skittering across water, which means anything is hard to recall, let alone a feeling from years ago, now worn away by time.

Maybe we were happy then, when we used to drink cappuccino or tea and share a flaky pastry. Above us, a sparrow hopped on vines, head turned upside down, sampling the grapes that shielded us from the light, her hand, birthmark stained, drawing a red grape too, the uproar of her laughter. We were both in love with something that day, whatever it was, the sunlight, the small statue, the playfulness of the birds. Those first heady months when everything about a person seems a wild discovery, a territory unmapped. Nostalgia is a siren song. And memory, changed by the passage of time as sandstone by river.

*

ON UNCERTAINTY

When I was a child in Chico, CA, we used to have drills where we'd huddle beneath our desks in preparation for a nuclear attack. I remember the windows in my small school room were impossibly high, and the teacher had to use a long metal pole with a hook on the end to unlatch them. This, unlike many memories, is not debatable. The windows were high, the pole, and the latch. Mr. Barnum with a pencil tucked behind his ear, impossibly old, probably thirty-two then, younger than me now, pushing them open, letting in the sounds of spring.

I recall curling, fetal, hands cradling my neck, trying to keep the imaginary debris from braining me, and, in my uncertainty, sometimes feeling as though the ceiling was falling, as though the very act of being under the desk would trigger the attack. Except, I am uncertain of this particular memory from 1988. In fact, I suspect we hid under our desks in preparation for an earthquake. And I'm conflating things in memory again, the vague fear of the USSR, which hovered at the edge of my conscious mind, pushed by Rocky films and *Red Dawn* has been superimposed over those earthquake drills. But I think we hit on a narrative truth in elementary school, cowering in fear. Disaster always sits at the edge of our life, territory unmapped, until it arrives as a thief in the night.

One thinks now, or perhaps just I think, of Stanislav Petrov, the Soviet military officer, who, when notified of an incoming nuclear attack from the United States by the warning system, declared the attack erroneous, likely staving off the start of a nuclear war. Petrov said he suspected the system was mistaken because he had been told to believe that the US would send five missiles, rather than one, which the system reported, alerting him, or at least highlighting that crucial factor, which underlies most complex thinking in this brevity amongst brevities, uncertainty, that doubt, like a child huddled beneath a desk, with only his imagination of the pain to come to keep him company. Where were you when I laid the foundations of the earth? Hiding.

*

My uncertainty in the relationship, which was sometimes a pleasure, a rich vein of daily thought, was all consuming. I was both uncertain about the relationship and uncertain if I could withstand its rupture. Running in parallel, as a line of tracks through the lonesome countryside, was a distrust of my uncertainty about the relationship, which seemed to be grounded, at least to my view then, in my selfish desire to inhabit two lives, two versions of self.

Once, ages ago, I memorized a poem by T.S. Eliot, and the refrain, *Life is very long*, keeps knocking through my head as sayings sometimes do, making themselves desperate to be heard. A thought reminds me of the years when I was in that relationship when I'd wake every morning with my subconscious mind beating like some horrendous drum. *You must decide what to do!* I am not a person who remembers dreams, so I was never certain if the voice led directly from the dream into the real world or whether it was just banging out a rhythm all night in the hope I'd figure it out.

And yet, I rarely thought about the necessity of making a decision about the relationship in my waking life, which was a cascade of packing healthy lunches for my children from the marriage, heckling them to brush teeth, to wake up on time, to eat healthy snacks, and then the balancing of jobs, of communicating with my ex, which meant that whatever spare time I came across was rarely spent trying to figure out something consequential on my own. As such, my subconscious mind ran amok, a Lynchian dream that I ignored on waking, dismissing as though it was a fortune cookie, a fate intended for another, Oedipus marrying without a thought.

*

Often my students at the university ask if I have an opinion about an article we've read for class. I sometimes tell them that I am uncertain of the argument myself. I say that I'm teaching the essay because I don't know what to make of the idea, whether it's brilliant or batshit. My classes are set up against the vast periphery of not knowing.

I ask my students what they think of a particular argument, Angela Davis on the coming replacement of housework, bell hooks on class consciousness, and we sit in silence, trying out uncertainty together. Why hasn't this world come to pass? They have ideas. I have some too. But after a while, I want to remind them that it's okay to not know yet, to fail at persuasion, to burn up, to shipwreck, to wander the garrulous green seas until you're hallucinating mermaids.

*

After a time, the central question of that relationship became whether we would move in together, buy a house, get married, have a child. And also, which neighborhood attracted us the most and how close we'd live to my ex. I suppose, when given an honest accounting, the question of the relationship was damn near everything, which movie to see, whether Michael B. Jordan had done a good job as an actor in a particular movie, whether to get pizza or tacos. Since our relationship was built on the edifice of uncertainty, any conversation could set off a crumbling, a sign that the earthquake would soon be in our midst, time to duck and cover.

What unnerves me then, about the presence of so much uncertainty, was not the weight of its presence, but rather, that it remained hidden for so much of my waking life, a Loch Ness Monster, unrealized, swimming beneath the murky depths of the day, Bigfoot lumbering through the massive redwoods. And yet, when I consider the relationship from a distance of a few years, it's crystal clear that the uncertainty was always present in my conscious world. It seems to me, at least on the surface of things, that these two statements cannot coexist, but are like oil in water. And yet, it's also clear to me that the way I've rendered it here is true. The uncertainty was both deeply present and almost entirely absent from my waking life. The mind doesn't work as we want it to. The mind works as it will.

*

Some psychologists argue that smartphones, Google Maps, easy access to technological data, knowing instantly who the starting quarterback was in Super Bowl VII or the Spanish word for banana, has left us even more anxious when we encounter uncertainty because we have become so used to easily banishing it, as though we had a light switch in an underground cave. Perhaps my long-term dalliance with uncertainty is or was one of my saving graces, an antidote to the certainty that prevails in every micro-climate on the internet. It is rare to hear someone doubt themselves on Twitter. Back then, I was certain of my uncertainty and thus, I thrived in it. Though now that I've written it, I see that it's a lie or at least an elision. Though to say that I was wholly unhappy in that uncertainty would also be a lie. I was unsteady, not unhappy. Or perhaps I was unhappy. Who's to say? Certainly not me, mired in the present moment, thinking of himself in the past as an object.

*

How did my partner tolerate my uncertainty? Although, I see now that it wasn't tolerated but endured. One of my favorite parts in the 3,600 pages of *My Struggle* novels by Karl Ove Knausgaard, is when he argues that the world isn't meant to be enjoyed but endured. It was precisely the sort of thing that my partner disliked about me. This fascination with enduring as opposed to joyously thriving. I resent it about my past self now too.

Although, in truth, what can we know of other human beings but what they self-report? And if what I reported to my partner didn't accurately represent my internal feelings, then it would be silly to assume that she reported her feelings accurately to me. And so on and so forth, in an infinite regress of mind wandering, like a ship spinning round and round before being sucked into the vortex.

*

The Bermuda Triangle is a mythic source of uncertainty. An area of disappearances, of planes disappearing from radar, of ships fading into the mists, of navigational systems run amok. In fact, Columbus claimed to have witnessed a great ball of fire passing into the ocean while traveling in the Bermuda Triangle, and later, an eerie light. Oddly, despite the numerous strange events, no one has determined that the Bermuda Triangle is particularly unsafe despite sightings of aliens, sea monsters, and underwater volcanic eruptions. However, the National Ocean Service classifies the area as normal. I'd like to think the Bermuda Triangle confirms the very start of this essay, uncertainty, disaster, not as things to fear but as realities.

*

Aristotle, a philosopher who would definitely have his own column in a major publication were he alive today, said that humans should use practical wisdom when dealing with uncertainty. The heart of practical wisdom is deliberation, careful thought. And yet, who has not lain awake in the depths of the evening trying to deliberate with their wild and fierce beating heart?

*

Scientists have linked emotional pain to physical pain, saying that the symptoms of emotional pain mimic those of the physical. Thus, the ruptures, the fights and short break-ups often felt awful, pit of the stomach painful, which is why we could never follow through with them. The misery was guaranteed either way, and any doubt of its veracity was immediately offset by the reality of these minor ruptures, which, by doubling and tripling the uncertainty we felt in one another's company, left us both swimming in the aftermath of an explosion we kept pretending hadn't happened as though the dinosaurs had kept walking about long after the meteor and ash had blotted out the sun's rays. How long can you survive without light?

*

Beyond the fear of nuclear war, my childhood was filled with stories of Bigfoot, of the Loch Ness Monster, of squids so giant they defied imagination. My own children don't have these stories to draw from, corollaries of the unknown from the natural world. Multiple times during my childhood, images of Bigfoot or the Loch Ness Monster would appear, and I felt myself excited by them. In a way, I suppose those monsters of yore foretold the age of disinformation. We were so desperate to believe in the unknown that we were willing to grasp any story if it confirmed our beliefs, calmed our uncertainty.

*

As the Scottish Philosopher David Hume pointed out, we have no guarantee that the sun will rise each day, but we still assume it will. Uncertainty is always hidden in plain sight. Perhaps that's why, no matter how difficult things got between us, we had faith that the sun would rise again in the morning of our relationship. We had faith that we'd argue at a coffee shop, marvel at the flavor of a blueberry muffin, put my children to bed with stories and then argue again over the plot of a television show.

*

The origin story of mermaids is a curious one. Sailors, after months on water, came across the wonder of manatees, and, in their uncertainty, saw beautiful women calling to them from the water. But imagine yourself, months at sea, listless and alone, when gauzy shapes glide through the azure water, sinuous and smooth, a wonder amongst wonders, something to distract from the scurvy. Those beautiful mermaids.

The siren too is a creature of uncertainty, half-woman and half-bird, not certain of either, living in hybridity, content in the folds of uncertainty. And yet, the promise only of a shipwreck to come, a meteor strike, the first trembling of an earthquake. The siren is an uncertainty as a creature but certain disaster. I think, in that last year together, we often heard the sound of the siren, but, tied to the ship's mast, blindfolded, we didn't know which way it was calling us, toward one another and disaster, or apart, and the same.

*

Months ago, I debated the merits of free will amongst friends and after several glasses of wine decided I'd rather drink whiskey than debate free will. But, free will, if it's your thing, implies a particular kind of uncertainty that makes, if my friend was to be taken seriously, life meaningful. Not just the illusion of choice, but choice itself is central to our conception of the human experience. And yet, in many ways, we're no fans of uncertainty. We'd like to know the weather, the quality of our children's school, the best recipe for coffee cake, where we should get good Thai noodles in our city and whether an actor we saw in an old movie was Burl Ives or not. Dwelling in uncertainty, once a prerequisite for fellowship amongst humanity, is no longer tolerated.

Oddly though, despite our tools of science, of big data measurement and quantifiable outcomes, uncertainty remains. The weather remains variable, snow sometimes falling in a boom or bust, the school ranking can shift rapidly if a principal and several good teachers leave, or our perception can change if our child has befriended a bad influence, the coffee cake can be a bit too sweet for our liking, 488 five-star rankings aside. Burl Ives remains Burl Ives, but I suppose we need some certainties like Burl Ives narrating to us about Rudolph or we'd all go insane. So how do we do it? How do we live in two places?

Not well.

ON UNCERTAINTY

*

For years, I'd been certain that we'd always remain in that uncertain state, on the cusp of breaking up, while never having the courage or fortitude to actually break up. It was an absurd dance, a certainty that we'd always remain mired in uncertainty. Thus, by paradox, creating the very conditions of our own almost indescribable misery, that of being with one another in uncertainty, while being certain that we'd remain that way.

*

The other touchstone of my childhood was a movie I watched over and over again, *The Neverending Story*. For years, I thought the character who played the young princess of a crumbling land was bald. When I referred to the movie, I often included this detail of its oddity, cataloging it as one more strange proclivity of that wild-eyed movie. Years later, when I watched the movie again, I realized she just had her hair tied back into a tight bun. Where had my mind generated the idea that she was bald? Why had those sailors thought of manatees as mermaids? Why are humans so strange?

But that isn't the only confounding thing about *The Neverending Story*. Rather, what boggles my mind is that the world wasn't being taken over by an evil villain, instead, it was being consumed by the nothing, an entity that was slowly devouring a world humans no longer believed in, a world of fairies and wolves, princesses and flying dog-dragons. The implicit argument of the movie, as told by that once bald princess, was that human beings, in their quest for scientific certainty, had forgotten about the fairies and dog-dragons, Loch Ness Monsters and Bigfoots, and that in forgetting those mythical beings, something had been lost. In retrospect, perhaps it was a movie about nuclear war or about losing out on your childhood. Maybe it was a movie about nothing.

*

Perhaps, were it not for Linnaeus, were it not for Mendeleev, we could bask longer in the sweetness of uncertainty, which has been banished. Imagine, just imagine, visiting a city as a complete stranger, giving yourself away to the streets folding, the dusky gold light accumulating on the streets wet after rain. What could you do with that uncertainty? Fixedness, certainly, is not erotic.

But certainty is sometimes what's desired, in a life, in an essay, a roadmap with which to make meaning, to plan a pit stop, find a place to pee. My brain has never worked that way though, at least not as long as I've known it. I suppose the future of my thoughts is unknown.

In my fiction classes, I tell my students time and again that the best endings are ambiguous, they are half-steps. Rather than knowing if the main POV character is a murderer, imply it without saying, leave the person hanging at the knife's edge of despair. What I'm saying is that we desire uncertainty, a door half ajar as opposed to closed.

*

My existential dread, long a sore subject in my relationship, feels infinitely weighted to that struggle. In fact, I had been religious for most of my twenties, and the falling out and loss of faith had precipitated big changes across the wide spectrum of my life. Without God, the ultimate certainty, I found myself adrift in a world that I conceived of as meaningless. It was that safe harbor, a loving God, that had long been a mooring point for the dread. When removed, life felt more like a cascade of water pouring over my head, like a shower in the morning, washing away my subconscious thought of what must be done about my relationship.

*

On our last night in Rome, we fought in front of the Trevi fountain, the banality of the fight, the beauty of the place. The night before, we'd both drunk too much and been invited to stay the night at a winery in the hills above Naples near the Amalfi Coast. As always, I wanted, no desired to stay there. We'd had several glasses of wine, figs, and fresh goat cheese, while the sun set over the bay, first pink, then a soft purple, then bright orange. The proprietor and his girlfriend asked if we'd like to stay, spend the night drinking with them in the wine cellar before sleeping it off at a property on site. I could not imagine a world in which we didn't take him up on the offer. We had nothing to get back to and the infinitude of a night on a quiet farm above the water awaiting us. We drove home.

On the drive home, we had a fantastic fight, berating one another as we threaded through the tiny villages on the Italian coast. I wonder, as the mind often does, how the night would have gone if we'd stayed in the hills, in the dark, drinking wine and laughing with strangers. In the morning, we woke to light glittering on the ocean, the cliffs and the small town of Amalfi below.

*

Most people don't love uncertainty, which is perhaps why so many people fear death, which looms, regardless of your stance on the afterlife, as the great uncertainty, the continuation of a lifelong grappling. Many people are certain that the afterlife exists. But people are also certain that Donald Trump had the election stolen and that 5G internet is designed to steal their identities, which is to say, humans are certain of many things. As for me, I take great comfort in my uncertainty. Certitudes strike me as banal, as ways of ending what's interesting about a story, about a life.

*

Before things ended, those years, for all their misery, were also tinged with a deep undercurrent of excitement that often rose and crested over us in the aftermath of a fight, in the indignity of me walking the streets in a drizzling rain after being asked to get out of her car, that rich promise as a tulip bulb planted in the fall, that one day, all our uncertainty would come to a culmination, as Trevi Fountain, or the Dome of St. Peter's, a final act that would justify the long years of work, of suffering. We could say we'd once stood together and marveled at the grandeur of Rome, the Dome striated in light, the square full of a sea of pilgrims, marveled too at the pillars framing the city below, the promise, amidst all that had already been dead and buried in that city, of something new arising from the rubble.

And then we parted.

On Being 35

I have a romantic temperament, which means I find no greater disappointment in life than myself—my dreams and ambitions unravel like thread as the years pass. I was going to be a professional basketball player, and I played for thousands of hours, trying to achieve the goal. I was going to be an excellent spouse, a traveler of the world, a counselor, and then a writer. That I am none of these things is largely the fault of my own, though sometimes I'll blame the gulf between my dreams and reality on the overenthusiastic parenting and teaching of the 80s and early 90s, and the adults who insisted you could be anything in the world if you set your mind to it. I could have set my mind to being a physicist from age 12, and I'd still have not reached it because I am God-awful at math. And in life, I cannot be excellent, only myself: a flawed being who spins out different versions of the self like a diamond refracting light.

That said, I am not an abject failure. I have several pleasing characteristics, for which, if I am lazy, I may be thankful. I am, by most modern conventional standards of the day, still an attractive individual. My nose is aquiline, Roman, and I have fairly deep brown eyes. My face is a bit too long, but I keep my hair short so as not to accentuate that fact. Women, on separate occasions, have complimented my full lips, expressive eyes, hair, and the shape of my eyebrows. No one has said anything about my ears, which may be sub-standard. This is not to say that I am unusually attractive because I am not. In fact, my relative attractiveness is a virtual non-sequitur when it comes to defining who I am. I had virtually nothing to do with shape or symmetry of my face, the depth of my eyes, or slant of my nose. My facial features and hair were largely determined at birth by genetics. I deserve some credit for my waist size because I have eaten carrots rambunctiously for decades, and I visit the gym regularly. Attractiveness, if one is intellectually rigorous, is not particularly laudable, nor a salve for my disappointment. One might as well compliment a turtle for having a shell.

I am, however, quite good at pleasing other people. I'm a good conversationalist, capable of moving between politics, art, the environment, and interpersonal relationships with ease. I am generally well-liked and nice to be around because I laugh often and listen intently. Perhaps, then, I should be proud of my ability to please. And yet, I can't take much credit for my nature because my overriding disposition to the world is one of desperately wanting to be liked. Thus, I engage in all sorts of contortions in thought, form, and spirit, all in order to achieve that goal— one moment a Christian, the next an atheist, a teetotaler and a binge drinker, a lover of sex and then abstinence, a believer in literature, movies, and a denier of art's possibility to change. These various costumes are often taken on and off more rapidly than those in a play, and though it's often to make others comfortable and happy, in doing so, I'm really pleasing myself.

I am athletic after a sort, capable of fielding sharply hit grounders and firing them across the infield with ease. I'm fairly fast and have always been able to shoot a basketball well.

Unfortunately, none of my athletic talents come within miles of world-class, which might make those talents middling at best. Besides which, I have nothing but genetics and a proclivity for playing video games in my youth to thank for my excellent hand-eye coordination. I do not mean to be immodest.

I am excellent at my time's tables and good at remembering numbers. This does not, unfortunately, put me on par with Mother Theresa or Sir Isaac Newton.

What am I, then, after 35 confusing years on the planet, besides skin stretched taut over bones?

I have developed one useful skill, I suppose, which is a sense of the aesthetics, an eye for the beautiful: the way that a tree, mid-winter, looks like a hand, and the English ivy growing up its limbs like a great green glove. I often spot the exact angle at which the window catches deep pockets of the sky, shades of blue and arcs of light. I can identify the difference between various styles of prose and elucidate the efficacy of an author's voice or its shortcomings, the complexities of character and narrative, which make an authorial move or character's decision pleasing in its symmetry. I can pick apart movies, actors' performances, and debate with intelligence the veracity of an earned ending. I am given to asking for silence at times with people I love, so that we can inhabit a moment: purple wisteria climbing a stone wall, a field of wildflowers bending in the wind, skeins of light on water, the water reflecting the sky, the trees, and if we listen closely as we look, the sound of birds in the thrush.

This is not to say my sense of aesthetics is unerring, but merely that it is the one thing I have come by honestly, my sense of the beautiful. Of course, perhaps none of the above is true. My sense of the beauty in narrative symmetry or excellent prose is not without repercussion. I received those ideas through years of schooling, and it's entirely possible those ideas are wrong, and certainly true that the ideas are skewed toward my own educational path. A person gathers so little knowledge in the space of one lifetime, who am I to proclaim my sense of aesthetics has been keenly developed? Particularly when tastes evolve as we age, like clouds taking new shapes across the sky.

THE BODY IS A TEMPORARY GATHERING PLACE

I can say with certainty, then, only that I enjoy travel and good books. And, in truth, neither of these pleasures are without problems. Enjoying travel is a love of the novelty, and novelty is the crutch of the lazy, an inability to experience the mundane as sacred. As for the books, well, as I've already said, I love what I love, and perhaps that's all any person can say. So let me tell you then of an afternoon when I was 26, staying at a small hotel in Florence, with my wife when we were happier.

I opened the old window from our hotel room overlooking the San Lorenzo Market. My shirt was off, and I stood there in my underwear, gathering in the morning as my wife implored me to close it. Below me, a collection of wooden carts were filling up the cobblestone streets, where soon tourists and Italians would pick through mountains of shoes, purses, belts—a kaleidoscope of color. To my left, looming over the tableaux, was the San Lorenzo Basilica, a church first built in 323 AD. Pigeons, iridescent-headed, bobbed and weaved like boxers on the steps. Brunelleschi and Michelangelo had a hand in the church, and the only nice thing a romantic failure like myself can say of Michelangelo is that eventually he died and made the rest of us stop feeling bad for how little we've accomplished.

For a minute or so, cool morning air flowed through the arched window, and I gathered in the moment, which is all we have in the end. The sun was warm on my skin, and the people were scattered like dust in the courtyard, and then it was gone. And off we went into the rush of the day, the small medieval streets of Florence, suddenly breaking open into a square full of light and magnificent stone statues, fountains of water, and tourists everywhere eating gelato and resting on sun-warmed stones and benches like cats. It was the day I first saw the *David*, the most magnificent work of creation I've ever seen, the white marble statue, somehow bigger in real life than one expects, the ribs and calves perfectly shaped.

I stood for a while in the Accademia, staring at the height of human creation. Until the crowd around me grew too great, my view temporarily obscured. And I washed out into the side corridors where other remains of statues lay on tables—stray elbows, heads without ears, fragments of fingers. And I felt a peculiar sense of being let down after seeing the *David*, amongst these small statues, which, if I am honest, have far more to do with my life and history than a statue gazed at by thousands daily. And I had a moment of recognition, all these years later: I am but a stray elbow, a portion of the upper ear, the remains of a pinkie finger, lying in a room off to the side, signifying nothing but what might have been.

On Showering and Mortality

After coffee, I stepped into the elevator and smelled the lingering scent of Suave and was transported back to childhood, into the small bathroom with yellowed tiles where I'd first learned to shower in the apartment my father shared with his second wife and family.

Smell is the sense most intimately tied to memory. The olfactory bulb runs from nose to brain, making stops in the amygdala and hippocampus, which is linked to forming memories. Thus, smell slowly permeates the thin web-like structures of memory. And now I am thinking of my father's impossibly large hands, the slightly large front teeth of his second wife, the low jet-stream of the shower.

I remembered the row of maroon carpeted steps that led up to the second floor of the apartment, where I used to race G.I. Joe's, dropping them headfirst from one step and seeing how far they'd tumble. I remembered the pungent odor of litter he kept in the master bedroom, and the way he seemed to always be folding laundry, wave after wave, hustling it along and folding it aggressively, exerting a kind of control he wished he had over everything.

The scent left me with an overwhelming sense of nostalgia, an almost physical pain for the past, for that child of eight, naked and cold. I did not want to be that precise child again, bossed and bullied at school, still frightened of the dark, of diving into the chlorinated pool, of father. Nor did I want to experience that summer again, which was full of swimming lessons in fractured light and cold winds, slow walks across the street, the long bend of a Wiffle ball tossed from father's hand or the slow leaching of light through the pear and lemon trees at my father's window as I spent hours playing video games.

What I found myself missing was not that particular childhood, but rather, the feeling of being a child, with all the doors of life open, sunlight pouring in every window. I wanted yet again to be rubbing a quarter-sized bit of shampoo into my hair, just as father had shown me, oblivious to the string of disappointments that comprise the shape of any adult life.

What might it be like to read *War and Peace* for the first time again? To kiss a girl? To wake up at 4am to watch the sunrise, to not know what an hour, what a day, what love or a life could possibly hold in its tremulous fingers? What might it be like to sink again, for the first time, into the warm hot tub in the silence of Castle Valley and stare up at the glittering stars?

It's a peculiar thing, aging. I often feel surprised by my reflection in a mirror or how many decisions of mine that have already been made: marriage, children, house, divorce. It's not so much that I've made poor decisions; who would trade the warmth of a baby's body curled into your chest? But rather, that so much time has passed, like water flowing swiftly beneath the hull of a fast-moving ship, the self, a prow.

My father was forty-one years old the day he explained how to shower to me. His voice, deep and stern-seeming because I saw so little of him, his hair was receding heavily, and his second wife was soon to leave him.

Today, I am forty years old, living a life that bears a resemblance to his, as though someone has sketched very poorly between one of those old dot to dot drawings. For like many children of absent fathers, I intended never to leave my children, until I left too, but then I stayed, two blocks up the road in a small apartment with a stained porcelain tub where my son, seven, sometimes showers.

The elevator plunged down, that vertiginous drop that is a bit like the twinges of love.

I don't remember what else happened that day, whether I ate cereal or built sandcastles. All I remember is standing on the fuzzy pink carpet, listening to my father, then pouring the quarter shaped dollop of shampoo into my hand, careful to get it exactly right. From here, I can still remember the smell of the shampoo, the silken green texture in the palm of my hand, the slow lathering of it through my hair. I can see the shape of things to come, once ragged and wild, now narrowing, now closing.

On Kissing

A first kiss, milestone among milestones. It doesn't mirror having sex for the first time. A kiss, especially a first kiss, is something else, a gateway, a rite of passage. We talked about virginity in high school, but that first kiss was something special, not forbidden, but yearned for, as Lancelot for Guinevere, as the Sumerian poet for their lover.

What of a kiss then? Why was I so scared? I'd like to say it's because I grew up in a Christian home, afraid of any physical touch, but I don't think that's true. I think I was terrified of rejection, of a turning of a cheek, of what it would mean for so much yearning to turn into nothing. And so I yearned without purpose, without something concrete as a goal, an inward journey that can never result in the thing itself.

An out of body experience, then, a kiss, something that transcends the humdrum nature of life. Not the cleaving off of the world in a kiss, but a unity. A loss of self, in self, a joining of the world, a harmonious symphony, which I'd recognize later when learning meditation. The way the universe, or just the little neat corner of mine in the quiet hills above the Pacific, briefly aligned, as our lips too, aligned. The sort of kiss that is more like a journey, a city sparkling below the curve of a plane's wing, all the promise of what's to come.

But which city, exactly? I suppose it had something to do with the anomaly of my age at that first kiss. Being kissed at nineteen is something quite different than being kissed at thirteen or sixteen, an age when everyone, or so it seemed to me, was being kissed. Bodies pressed against lockers after school, hands held after class, the way everyone made out before saying goodbye. The electric undercurrent of adolescence, charged with desire.

So backward, then, to that moment. The first time I kissed someone, I was eighteen years old. Or nineteen. It was near my birthday, holiest of days, and memory blurs. An embarrassing age, I admit. She and I were almost dating then, an embarrassing thing to have never dated either. We should have kissed weeks prior, long after she'd made clear how she felt about me, but that old familiar fear, of rejection, of the uncertainty that folds itself into any human interaction. Unsure then as we strolled around the walkway of how or whether she'd enjoy it. Whether I'd, so unsure, reveal myself as I was, inexperienced and scared, and not as I projected. That old human conundrum, distances between who we are and what we imagine. Then our faces bent together, a kiss.

After I kissed someone for the first time, I walked up the hill at our small Christian college in Montecito, CA, the rich, tree-swathed and vastly gated community where Oprah lived just above Santa Barbara. The campus was lined by sprawling oaks, small shrubs, a campus that would burn profusely in the never-ending California wildfires, such that the densely thicketed college where I attended no longer exists, but has been replaced by one of thinner trees, sparser shrubs, more corridors of light.

But the real point, digression aside, was that I felt, after the kiss, as though I was floating, ethereal, as close to spirit as I'd get on my Christian campus. Not a kiss, then, but something that changed my life. Whatever abyss had lain behind me, the embarrassment of never having kissed someone was now in the rear-view mirror. I had been kissed. The future was unfolding.

The walk that night, uphill, coastal breeze, not the Santa

Ana winds, which are warm and are said to bring on craziness and fires. So cold, salt-tinged. But being briefly out of my body it's hard to catalogue the weather with any sort of precision, as I was in the weather, not outside of it. We kissed along the pathway, past the building that housed the university president and provost's office, past the tiered garden with the magnificent orange and blue Birds of Paradise, beak like flowers slowly beginning to awaken. On the slow curve of driveway, we paused. I may have mentioned the moon to her, noticed it between the interlocking branches of two oaks, nervous.

*

The first recorded kiss, though certainly not the first kiss, comes from the Vedas, Sanskrit Scriptures around 3,500 years ago. Kissing then, unlike nuclear war and climate disaster, not a recent invention, but a slow unfolding through time. In fact, discoveries of a microbial genome in Neanderthals' gums suggest that they were sharing food or perhaps kissing humans. Kissing then has always been foundational to the human experience.

Kissing is described in Sumerian poetry and surviving Egyptian love poetry. As soon as humans could write, they wanted to write about kissing. The Sumerian:

> And when her lips are pressed to mine
> I am made drunk and need not wine.

We humans, and perhaps Neanderthals, not just taking a roll in the hay, but rolling tongues, pressing lips. See also, swapping spit, sucking face, a peck, a smooch, necking, making out, lip smacking, tonsil hockey.

But when was the real first kiss? Our proverbial Adam and

Eve. Perhaps it's best to pause first on the oddity of kissing, heretofore assumed as central to the human experience, poetics and Neanderthal remains attesting to it. Not every culture kisses on the lips. Less than half, in fact, a study done by a group of Scottish scientists on 168 different cultures concluded. Clothes, it turns out, tend to make people kiss on the lips more often. Some nibble on the eyelashes in lieu of kissing. Others take a quick whiff of one another, which makes sense given the recent research on pheromones and attraction. The hiding of erogenous zones, meaning this Anglican body of mine was starved for lips by being bereft of uncovered skin.

In the past, emperors have banned kissing, thinking it only the proper province of the powerful. Kissing has also been banned during times of disease. So if only I could time travel back and tell my younger self that a kiss is merely a construct amongst other constructs, a shadow thing, not the passage from childhood into the throes of adolescence. But perhaps that means a kiss is nothing and everything at the same time, a thin line across two gorges. In short, one cannot escape the time they are born into. If only I'd known that a kiss isn't really a kiss, a borderland between two worlds. And yet, it was. And whether that was cultural, the product of movies and pent-up desire, doesn't matter. A kiss is both a construct and a portal into another world. We live in simultaneity. A kiss is everything. A kiss is nothing.

*

Years pass. No dawdling about with years as you see with days. This was after the kiss, after the marriage, a rainy day in Paris, low scrim of sky. A brief discussion about what to do with the day, I'm convinced I'd like to see sculpture. I still remember the majesty of Florence, the *Pietà*, the breathtaking majesty and exquisite curve of the *David*. The incredible precision of the Ghiberti doors, which had stunned me, that such works could come from human hands. An absurdity akin to the earth itself. We wander through the voluptuous statuary outside of the Rodin Museum, bronze statues arrayed in various poses of pain. The rain slackens, rays of light falling, sky gone gauzy. The rain somehow still falling occasionally, a sun shower, statues bathed in light.

I take a picture next to *The Thinker*, thinking myself, wander over to *The Gates of Hell*, take a closer look at where I'm headed if mother is right. By way of Dante, "Abandon every hope, who enter here." Bit dark, I think. Inside the museum, after the pictures and the marveling at the statues, more Rodin. More of his statues, and the agonizing sculptures, bodies contorting in grief, of his lover, Camille Claudel. Do you imagine Rodin and Claudel kissing? Yes, many times. His gargantuan and sensuous sculpture, *The Kiss* memorializing the lust shared between Paolo and Francesca, so moved by the story of Lancelot kissing Guinevere, unable to contain themselves, banished to hell. Dante here:

> Pause after pause that high old story drew
> Our eyes together while we blushed and paled;
> But it was one soft passage overthrew
> Our caution and our hearts. For when we read
> How her fond smile was kissed by such a lover,
> He who is one with me alive and dead
>
> Breathed on my lips the tremor of his kiss.
> That book, and he who wrote it, was a pander.
> That day we read no further.

I have always loved that line, that day we read no further. As Virgil and Dante talk to Francesca, the reader is meant to understand the weight of their sin, of their guilt, the strange geometries between guilt and my own childhood fear of a kiss. And yet, when I read the line, that day we read no further, I too, am filled with desire, creating a triplicate of desire, from Lancelot to Guinivere, from Paolo and Francesca through to me, the reader, who before he had kissed anyone, used to read, in secret, the pages of fantasy books where kisses were shared, desire lovingly described. How much of a kiss, of desire, exists outside of the act itself? How does a kiss move from a simple act into something that transcends, that immortalizes, as Francesca and Paolo.

*

Kissing releases oxytocin, serotonin, dopamine, a cocktail of things that made me feel that tightrope walk, that floating on air. Dare I say Euphoric? The word I always use when telling my students what I think Zadie Smith is referring to in her essay on Joy. Was that the feeling? How many times have I felt it since? The radical dissolution of self into the world.

The kiss was sloppy. Having not kissed, I had always been too embarrassed to ask for any advice on kissing. I'd imagine, though I cannot confirm, that I'd probably kissed my own arm before, tried out just what made applying one's lips to something so alluring. The tenderness of skin, soft brush of lips. And these kisses of my arm were more like conjectures than kisses and taught me nothing of lips, or more accurately here, what to do with the tongue.

If I were going for feats of skill, I should have asked a giraffe, possessor of a one-foot tongue. And giraffes do, sometimes kiss, wrapping tongues around one another, a massive tug of war. But mostly, which is why I'd never ask, giraffe tongues are for the seizing of acacia leaves, for reaching those sweet things to munch and crunch. Not to kiss then. In relation to its body size, the chameleon has the longest tongue in the world. But a chameleon is not famous for its ability to kiss, but rather, for using its nimble tongue as boomerang, for the catching and swallowing of insects.

Elephants put their trunks in one another's mouth. Dogs lick one another, nether regions too. And why not, what other way to pass the time? Bonobos, our famous horny cousins, give long and romantic kisses between sessions of self-stimulation. Chimpanzees, so alike in spirit to us they even engage in murder, give long French kisses of the sort I thought I was giving that night.

Honeybees kiss, of a sort. After spending the day collecting nectar, a frolicsome buzz among purple phlox, spikey coleus, dog-eared coneflower, they store the sweet bounty in their stomachs. When they return to the hive, punch drunk on nectar, another bee sucks the nectar from their mouth in something that appears to be a kiss. But sometimes, I hope, a particularly rambunctious worker bee takes it upon itself to sit with the sweet nectar in the belly, to idle in the garden, doze for a bit, drunk on the bounty of the world as I was that night, as the poet was millennia ago.

But enough of drowsing bees, nectar-filled. What I felt as I walked up the hill, bruise of sky overhead, was the pathway opening, a new way of seeing the world. Thinking now of Jean Francis Gravelet, netless as he tightrope walked across Niagara Falls. Gravelet balanced in the eyes of all who watched him, those who had taken bets on whether he'd fall. On one side, death; on the other, a kind of immortality. For me, a tightrope walk from one stage of life and entrance into another, brighter. The other side. A freefall into adulthood, pleasure.

*

Two summers after the kiss, twenty-one then, beers with friends in the deadening heat of a valley summer, star thistle choked hills, dusty live oaks, streets so warm the tar sometimes began to melt. Home. I told a friend that day, briefly in between one relationship and another that I'd like to kiss one hundred girls before I get married. He seemed impressed, a quick smile. He was the sort of person I'd looked up to during high school, brash and confident. He called his parents by their first name.

I realized then that I've overplayed my hand, let the moment have the better of me. One hundred, what an absurd number. I was taken for a moment by the spirit of what I'd missed, the hotel rooms after prom, the press of lips to skin. Silly, I supposed, even in the moment, a stupid goal. Better to be one of those bees that lay lazily in the clover than a young man drinking his own wish fulfillment as though it were wine.

But now to tug the thread back to fourteen. Fourteen then, living in the star thistle town. A college town, but really, a cow town. The smell of rice fields burning after the harvest, acrid smell sometimes reaching into the town itself. No sign of a life outside of the oaks and sycamore, the parties I don't get invited to. Lonely then, but now I see through the window of time, somewhat by choosing. How my friends kept inviting me over to spend time with girls, and I said I'd rather play a video game. Always oppositional, even then, driven away from what others want me to do. And yet, perhaps more too, something like fear of what was to come.

Or perhaps, by way of a detour, to follow the thread all the way, my grandmother, Margaret, used to always peck both of my cheeks whenever I arrived at her house. Did she kiss the air? The mind can't seem to grasp her fully, just her laughter, ever present, the way she chastised her son, my father, when he was too mean to the children. An apple-cheeked woman, four feet and eleven inches, serving salami and fresh apple juice. Margaret.

Her son, my father, who sometimes kissed me too, a surprise of bushy mustache. A father you didn't see all that often, the surprise of his kiss. What does a kiss from a distant father mean? Perhaps more than that of a lover. I kiss my children every night before bed.

The tumble of days, warp and weft of memory, but the job of the essay is to weave them back together, to say that summer I was fourteen and trapped in star thistle town, kissless, dreamless, and lonely, I saw a movie. The magic of pop culture, the moment before Jessie and Celine kiss in *Before Sunrise*, the way they awkwardly look away, not quite catching one another's glance. The way, years later, I'd mention the moon held in the curve of oak. And, in truth, this will always be, except when I'm drunk and bold, the way that I kiss someone, not a quick rush, but something protracted, a quiet dance, long after I should have, as a bee before it alights on the sex of a flower.

The upside-down kiss in *Spiderman*. The first kiss between Wesley and Buttercup in the *The Princess Bride*. Julia Roberts telling Richard Gere in *Pretty Woman* that she'll do anything but kiss on the lips. Tom Hanks and Meg Ryan in *Sleepless in Seattle*. The end of every romantic comedy I watched in the nineties. A kiss as signifier, as ending.

Romeo and Juliet at just the right time. Though more a memory of a field trip to San Francisco that I balked at going on to see *Phantom of the Opera*. Oh, the mistakes of my misspent youth! No kissing and no opera? Cow towns. But the sudden magic of watching Olivia Hussey as Juliet, fourteen and madly in love with her in that black and white film of a play no one in our class liked. But Olivia Hussey, still bright in memory, the way film captures a moment in a life and memorializes it.

Olivia Hussey, forever bent on the balcony, cleavage beckoning, calling wherefore art thou, Romeo? Teenage boys watching her in the small classroom, riven with desire.

And time elongates again. Not getting anywhere close to one hundred kisses. An absurd goal anyway. Losing track after ten or so, then the number fixed by marriage, by the birth of children. Then the brief period of dating after things end. The number rising swiftly again but not much interest in it now. A pressing of lips, electric, yes, but not tight rope walking, not the sense of a world suddenly cracking open, not a beginning, but something closer to an ending.

I'd like to wander then, through the folds of memory back to the place where kissing began, take another turn around that oval-shaped walkway beneath a sky scarred by stars, pause beneath the majestic oaks bending into one another, then our bodies, then mouths, everything moving in concurrence, like a symphony, like the beginning of something I'll never quite grasp again but always yearn for.

On Baths

I lost a lot of things in the separation: a house, a side yard I'd planted with woodland phlox, purpling ground cover, honeysuckle sliding up the old cable wire, bees drowsing in summer heat, the dresser that held my jeans and old sweatshirts, a shared bank account, and a couch that wasn't a futon, but what I miss most tonight is the glorious bath. The tub was porcelain, and the tap was delectably slow, hot water crept up at a snail's pace, warming my body inch by inch while the rich thrum of the fan drowned out the sound of the children, of traffic, of the creaking oak floors. I was cradled by the water, comforted by the wind.

If I'm given enough time alone, I start to brood over life's incongruities, my mind fixates on the particularities of my life, picking it apart piece by piece, but I'm soothed when I'm fully immersed in the water, feeling alone, but content. Something about the warmth—or maybe it's just a reminder of the womb, no matter how old I am—quiets the pitter patter of idle thoughts. My apartment has a bath too, but it's smaller, and the hot water always gives out before too long, and I am only half-covered by the water, discontent, wondering whether it's worth the twenty-minute wait while the pipes warm.

*

The father of the essay, Michele de Montaigne, thirty-eight, the same age as me, retired from his public life to Bordeaux, tired of its obligations. The parallels end there, as I have only recently started my career path, around the same time Montaigne left his. In his retirement, beyond inventing the essay, Montaigne suffered from kidney stones, and he often stopped at baths on his European travels, hopeful that the ache would disappear in the healing waters. One imagines him lying there, this French aristocrat, nearly doubled over in pain, waiting in vain on a bit of warm water to ease his pain, hopeful as we all are, for something miraculous to happen. Montaigne's pain never went away, but his skepticism about baths grew. He saw that only foreigners were healed, and he understood, without knowing it yet, the placebo effect.

*

I was at the ruins of Pompeii this summer, that famous Roman villa annihilated in a single day by the eruption of Vesuvius, which covered the city in piles of molten ash, extinguishing the dreams and stories of two thousand lives. The bodies are preserved in plaster casts, which take the shape of mummified horrors, people holding hands to their heads or crouching in the doorway. The plaster was poured into the hollow space that bodies left in the ash, and when the casts hardened, some of the bones were locked away in them as well. In the distance was the blackened top of Vesuvius, still glowering over the remarkable remains of the city as though it were an ancient and whimsical god. There is something in disaster which attracts the human spirit, some recognition of our own frailty, which we so often deny.

We were listening to a guidebook about the city as we wandered by the public baths there, unique for the sexually explicit images that were painted in the men's and women's dressing rooms—threesomes and various other sexual contortions. We couldn't find the blocks, or perhaps they had all been hauled away to a museum nearby, and the baths, as they often do, just looked like an empty grassy knoll, and it was left to our imagination to fill in the mosaic tiles and Romans bending down to lift water onto their backs, but I suppose the better part of life is being able to imagine the lives of others, which I often fail at.

*

As a child, I loved baths, loved the way my body felt so light, loved the way I could fashion soap bubbles into a robust beard, loved the way I was cordoned off in a world of childish fantasy while my mother tended to the house. I was free to push cars along the white enamel rim of the bath, conjuring thunderous tsunamis with the wave of a hand, free to conduct fierce fights between my G.I. Joe's, free to exult in being alone, the world, which held its own sadness, like my departed father and sad mother, held at a remove from whatever I imagined.

As I grew older and everyone else transitioned to showers, I still bathed, still sat in the scalding hot water until it had gone lukewarm, reading fantasy books about magical elves, dazzling swordfighters, and cauldrons full of dead men. I loved the way that a book's spine bent easily in my hand and the way the fan kept the world of puberty, of video games, of robust sexual fantasies and furtive masturbation, briefly at bay. I was embarrassed that I still took baths, but I couldn't stop myself. Like many teenagers, I felt that my life was fundamentally different than everyone else's, and I wanted to hide that from them, while still retaining the childish pleasure of a warm bath or a long walk around the neighborhood with my mother.

Time passed as time is wont to do. I got married, bought a house, had two children, checked the boxes of a good American life. My course seemed set, like the laying of bricks on a Roman road, one day passing into another. It was easy to imagine retiring into a life of reading classics in the tub, Dickens, Tolstoy, and a glass of a medium-bodied Italian wine waiting in the kitchen. And then I lost it. Any life can veer off course, stirred by the same childish whims that once produced storms in a bath, and then life is something new, something that has lost its shape, and I'm now bending words by myself in an apartment. But that isn't this particular essay. This essay is about baths.

*

The Romans made bathing into a fashionable spectacle, a place to see and be seen. Like most great Roman ideas, it was cribbed from the Greeks and made into something more lavish, more suited to the rise in their living standards, the ornate tiles in many of the houses in Pompeii far surpass the boring white walls in most modern houses. The Roman baths were spread throughout the empire, tracing the advance of the legions. The baths closer to Rome, like the one I half-saw in Pompeii, were legendary, mosaics adorned the floors, marble walls gleamed, and columns held up the roofs of fire-proof terra cotta bricks. Long furnaces ran beneath the floors, super-heating the water on its way to the baths, an impressive feat of architectural engineering in the service of human pleasure, that oldest of pursuits.

*

After the separation, I made a vow to travel once a year to Europe alone. My own father started traveling a few years back after inheriting some money at the death of his mother. Now we're both traveling the world on solo trips, seeing the world anew, but he's still hard to imagine sometimes, my father.

There are the ruins of baths in nearly every city I've visited. In southern Spain, the baths were a remnant of the Ottoman Empire, and I stood in those baths in Granada, taking pictures of a circle of blue sky overhead. In truth, though I can't imagine the baths as anything, I still pay to visit them, stamping my life with an approved touristic experience, even though I abhor the word tourist and call myself a traveler. My father tours in groups; I travel. I haven't quite found what I'm looking for in life or in the baths throughout Europe, but I keep following the same well-worn paths—travel, freedom, tropes of a new life—as if I am looking for a second, secular baptism, hoping that the right path appears sometime, and I can walk down it toward something like a public bath, naked bodies clothed in water and light.

I traveled to Budapest this summer, the Hungarian city that's known for its baths, a former communist city, boring and blocky, that has become a playground for partiers where people wander between ruin bars, swilling beer and looking for drugs. I snapped pictures of Vajdahunyad Castle, ivy creeping up its stony side, pleasure boaters paddling on the reflecting pool across from it. I walked across the Szechenyi Chain Bridge at midnight, capturing the stunning Hungarian Parliament, Fisherman's Bastion, regal and white, and the whole of the city aglow across the mirror of the Danube. Those pictures are from the first night, when the place I was staying was full of drunken revelers, people who looked like homeless pirates, and my bed didn't have a sheet on it yet. I'd just traveled eighteen hours, and I couldn't imagine spending the night surrounded by drunk Brits and Americans trying to drink their way through Europe. After taking pictures for two hours, I walked home across the bridge and toward my neighborhood, and every two blocks a woman appeared from the shadows and said hello. It took me three or four hellos to realize the women were prostitutes, and I stopped saying a cheerful hi back and hustled home through the darkness.

I flew out a day later, on my way to Amsterdam and then Prague, but when I returned to Budapest a few days later, I was eager to see the city with fresh eyes. The world had been returned to me in the days in-between, and the myopia with which I'd viewed the full range of human experience, drunken or not, had passed away. I'd been reminded of the beauty, the silliness, and the confusion of human life, dancing on a stage in Prague, or wandering the streets after eating a brownie in Amsterdam, reminded that I wasn't above anyone, even drunken piratic people, whatever pretensions I clung to. But first, I needed a bath.

The Gellert Baths in Budapest were founded in the thirteenth century, when King Andrew put a hospital at the base of Gellert Hill and pitched the baths as restorative for the wounded. Montaigne would have been skeptical, but he had the good sense not to have been born yet. The Ottoman Empire eventually captured Buda and installed a complex of baths of their own, which were later destroyed as well. There were attempts to revive the baths throughout history because everyone seems to love a good warm soak as much as they love destruction.

The Art Nouveau structure that makes up the current Gellert spa and baths is only a hundred years old. The exterior has a rounded dome, and the complex has ten different pools, an impressive interior adorned by marble columns, a wave pool for kids, steaming saunas, and a frigid pool. In the warming pool, gargoyles spit warm water over the backs of old Hungarians, which fractures off them, as though they are possessed with wings of water.

If the baths were once constructed for healing, I needed it. I was in the throes of a break from a tempestuous relationship and freshly released from the academic year where I have two jobs and precious little time to myself. My downtime is usually spent correcting thesis statements and dreaming up new ways of describing critical thinking to eighteen-year-olds. The week had been long—five flights, long nights of alcohol-fueled conversations, days of threading through the magical streets of Prague, walking along the canals of Amsterdam, brisk and gleaming waters—solitude, connection, loneliness, beauty. Gellert was the ur-bath, an attempt to wash everything away, the life that I'd traveled here with and the life that I'd been living here, which couldn't last. I should tell you that I'm always reading the "Archaic Torso of Apollo"; I am always trying to change my life.

How long do you have to stay warm before everything starts to change? Montaigne could have warned me, as I sat outside in the mildly warm outdoor pools, the yellow façade of the baths framing a rectangle of blue sky, curtains of clouds, that life doesn't change in an instant, that it takes days, weeks, years, for the new self to emerge.

Besides which, I had a return flight. And the flight dictated that I'd land and be thrust back into the life with its myriad of complications that I'd constructed over the last three decades and mangled in a way that vaguely reminded me of my own childhood, my own absent father.

*

And so, earlier tonight, three weeks after my travels had ended, I was lying in the shallow lukewarm suds of my bath. I'd added Epsom salts to assist with the aching in my aging knees, worn cartilage from years of basketball, waiting for the water heater to kick in again. I was weary with the strictures of life, of shuttling the children off to school, then hopscotching through traffic across town to work, two hours of commuting—a slog through the Columbia Heights neighborhood in D.C., backtracking, honking, listening to short story podcasts, philosophy bites, attempts to capture meaning in the day, trying to slip through side streets, only to be foiled by a van, or construction, and all the drivers trying to pass through the narrow streets that come together like tributaries to form a river. I rage until I arrive at work, cutting off the last strands of an interview where a writer is talking about the permutations of a short story they love. I suppose I should take some small pleasure in the way we are all united on that morning commute, all wishing we were somewhere else.

In the evening, I roast broccoli, heat chicken nuggets, put apples on the table while the children shovel food in and watch something PBS-approved that teaches them a lesson about kindness or the value of persevering. After dinner, I remind them to clear the dishes, elbows deep in the sink's water, never sitting myself, as I prepare their meals for the coming day: stuffing snap peas into containers, sunflower seeds, dried cranberries, sandwiches, hummus for one child, SunButter and jelly for the other. Dad, they keep saying, as if they are babies again, just learning the word, trying to direct my attention to cards, to cars, to a drawing they've done, or something interesting they saw at school. And now my hours are limited, so I say yes, time and time again, bending over to peer at pictures, to vroom cars across the floor until I am wrung out like a towel.

Which is why I want to lie in the unsatisfyingly lukewarm bath as if it is a cave at the end of the world. I want to wander Europe again, taking photographs of mountains reflected in lakes, to ruminate on butterflies whirring round the vineyard below a monastery in Prague, or marvel at the leaves whirling in small tornadoes beneath a windmill in Amsterdam. In the bath, I read a book of quiet essays about nature—peat moss, flowers touched by pebbles of rain. From the distance, I hear my daughter calling out, dad, dad, dad, dad.

*

The moss is still growing around the baths of Caracalla in Rome. At its height, the baths built during the second century included a small windmill, two libraries, one for Latin books and one for Greek, and an enormous window that looked out on the tableaux. And this contents me, knowing that two thousand years ago everyone else was sitting round in the warm baths turning the pages of books to pass the time, mulling over the vagaries of life.

*

My daughter is an anxious sort, perhaps pulled apart by the separation, forced to stretch her slender psyche between two houses like a rickety bridge spanning canyon walls. She learned about rabies and asked questions for hours, wondered if she'd get it and die, asked about the shots, about whether animals in D.C. had it. She approaches me daily, brow wrinkled with sincere concern: I ate a soap bubble; I breathed in some smoke; I think I accidentally ate a pom pom frond; Can I die from that? At first, I try to reassure her quickly. No. No. Not from that. When it goes on for days, I start telling her she has thirty seconds to live, then I slowly begin to count.

Once, when she was much younger, and we all still lived together, I told my daughter a story before bed that went like so—there was a daddy squid who lived in the sea. When the day was over, other fish kept talking to him, and he got tired. He sprayed ink into the water and slipped down and down into the depths of the ocean until he faded away. She leaned toward me sleepily, and

I repeated down and down into her ear as my own eyes closed, whispering it like an incantation. The daddy squid went down and down and down and down and down and down and down and down and down and down and down and down and down and down and down and down until no one could find him.

What I want my daughter to remember—this little rope of bunched muscle—are the mornings I was there when she was very young and she swam to me, round, fat, and pink, and I gathered her in like gold.

We were in a swimming class together months after she was born, and she had balls of doughy flesh gathered at her knees and elbows, protruding from her little pink bathing suit. When I stepped outside with her cradled in my arms, I saw row upon row of mothers cupping babies to their chests. I stood at the edge of that lonely stretch of blue, knowing I was an intruder. Mercifully, the teacher encouraged me to get in.

The water was cold, and I felt like the ugly duckling. I stared right at the teacher or right at my daughter. I was aware if I looked around I'd feel more out of place, or the women there would think I was trying to stare at their chests, or Sadie would think I was going to drop her in the water. I focused on the baby and the cold. We were told to hold the babies away from us, and she started to cry. I gathered her up in my right arm, holding her fleshy body against my chest. She was so warm. She batted the water with her ham-like fist, lifting droplets into her face, which astonished her each and every time, her blue eyes, now brown, shot through with wonder. We never went back to the lessons. But I hope somewhere a shred of that day remains, her father holding her, droplets of water clinging to her long eyelashes.

I still remember the swim lessons my father took me to and the outdoor pool that was so frigid in the early summer. He stood at the edge of the pool, but I don't remember if he encouraged me or merely passed the time.

When my daughter was first born, we gave her baths in the kitchen sink. When she was slightly older, we moved her out of the sink and into a small white tub that we rested on the kitchen table. The first time we tried to give her a bath there, we forgot to plug the hole in the bottom properly, and the water quickly drained away, soaking the oaken table and floor. My daughter screamed and screamed, her mouth flaming crimson as she screamed at the cruelty of whatever the hell it was that we were doing to her.

My father didn't have a proper bath in his room in the apartment, so I eventually started taking showers. I remember standing there in my towel while my father taught me that you only put a quarter's worth of shampoo into the palm of your hand, that a little goes a long way. I retain that memory until this day, thirty-one years later, and I tell my own children something similar about the shampoo, how they only need a small amount to wash their hair.

*

The early Christian baptism included a full immersion in water, the idea that not only were sins washed away, but that the soul was born anew. After Christ's baptism, the Holy Spirit descended in the form of a dove. My baptism in the Catholic Church was a mere sprinkling of water on the forehead, a consecration to a God I no longer believe in.

*

As my daughter grew, I gave her more baths myself, and I had to invent elaborate games to pass the time while she soaked in the tub. This time gave birth to Mr. Froggerton, a small green hand puppet who was prone to getting in trouble. The puppet had an English accent for some reason, and he loved to describe his stories of narrowly escaping large birds of prey, darting beneath the water, threading through the children's legs or passing over their hair in the madcap adventure to save his life. Most days he made it out safely, and the children would want to talk to the hand puppet, giggling at the way he called them both love.

Later, when I was tired and disengaged, and the children begged for Mr. Froggerton, I'd end the story more quickly, saying something like, and then the falcon eviscerated Mr. Froggerton and spilled out his entrails, the end. The children objected to this particular ending, not because he died, but because the story was so short. Tell it again, they'd say.

Mr. Froggerton is gone now, banished to the bathtub two blocks away, but the memory of him still lives on, such that whenever my son hears a British accent he asks after the puppet, as though all British people know Mr. Froggerton well.

*

My tepid bath, disappointing though it may be, was an escape into my own time—time which evaporates into a world of snacks, ice packs, screen time allocations, inane games like Chutes and Ladders, and idle encouragement of nearly everything—art, spelling, defecation. I am tired of admiring the particular shape of feces, of the squiggly lines of sunshine in the corner of a picture of a mom and dad who are no longer together. What I want is to sit in lavish silence and brood, ungratefully, on what life has brought to me as though I have had very little role in shaping things, which is wrong, but a belief I cling to, naively, stupidly, fiercely.

I wonder after my own father then, standing at the edge of the pool, watching four of his six children take lessons, wonder if he knows how he shaped his own life or whether he too feels that something overwhelmed him. I suspect that we're not so different, he and I, no matter how many barriers I sometimes try and put between us.

*

At Gellert, I lay in the quiet of the afternoon and gazed at the tableaux of thin clouds, birds wheeling overhead, and the blue meaningless sky. I had lain awake most of the night before, awash in memory and sorrow. I kept waiting for the wave of tiredness and sadness to break as though the bath could cleanse me of everything. I wanted the sun and water to melt me down to my constituent parts so I could be rebuilt again.

*

Soon enough, my daughter's voice swayed me. I folded the book down and placed it next to the bath. She was frantic then, lightly crying, and I lay next to her in the dark. She calmed down and told me a wild story, so happy for presence. Fatherhood is easy. It's just being there, and then being there again, and again, and again, and again, and again, ad infinitum. What could be easier than presence?

While my daughter and I lay there, my phone beeped. I had a text, and I slid my phone from my pocket and let the glow fill the room, eager to be elsewhere. My daughter was relating a series of puns she'd read in a magazine: why did the cow cross the road? He wanted to go to the mooovies, and I tried to laugh, desperate for the interaction to end, for the silence to return.

THE BODY IS A TEMPORARY GATHERING PLACE

What am I so desperate to get back to, to brooding at the edge of the bath?

*

By 500 AD, the baths at Caracalla, once one of the seven wonders of Rome, were in ruins. The baths at Gellert were only one hundred years old after having fallen into disrepair, and the baths in Granada were only remnants, red bricks, green grass, everything come to ruin.

*

At Gellert, the new friends I've come with tumble out of the super-heated sauna and into the frigid cooling pool. Earlier, in a daze from lack of sleep and tending my sadness, I'd lost them both for over an hour, wandered the complex, checking in every room, the warm pool, the hot pools, the outdoor pools, desperate to find them. But now I know where they are, and I sit in the warm outdoor waters, the sky a cathedral of blue overhead, and I breathe in and out, very deeply, as time thrums on, just as the fan once did when I was a child.

Montaigne died at the age of fifty-nine, which meant he spent twenty-one years essaying, in search, through words, for meaning. Everyone knows that the origin of the word essai is attempt, but no one wants to attempt something, they want to succeed.

*

I am nearing forty years old myself, the halfway mark of a contemporary life. After I leave my daughter's room, I sit on the edge of the tub, eyeing the tepid water. I wonder over the shape of the years to come, what the children will make of the life before them and if they'll make, as I have, something less of it than it should be. I want to slip into the bath and read with the intensity I once did as a child, shutting out the world, but the water isn't warm enough. I pull the plug and watch the water drain away, exposing the white enamel, stained by small spots of rock salt from when I'd left our snowy shoes in it last winter, one more ruin. I sit on the edge of the tub, bone-tired, naked, and alone.

III

This Essay Is About Everything

My old professor, the writer Richard McCann, once said, "an essay can only be about one thing." This essay is about everything. Not because it's a provocation, but because life, goddamn life, isn't ever about one thing. It's about the music you're listening to while driving your kids to camp. It's about the small patches and low places in the road; the broken yellow lines of paint; the brakelights of a beige Toyota Yaris; whether you love your kids enough; whether you're on time to work; whether you've got a passport ready for your trip to Montreal; and that's just a moment in time that elides the line of oaks, slivers of sunlight on the road, the rows of Tudor Houses, and the large green bushes that you know are azaleas because, come spring, the street is alive with pinks, whites, purples, butterflies, and bees. And that moment blooms into one after another after another. That's life. An essay can only be about everything.

The light in my one-room apartment is brilliant in the morning between seven and eight. The sunlight scissors through the sky, making geometries on my furniture, leaving other parts—a bookcase, a rug—as islands of shadow. The blinds are up in my apartment as they usually are.

One of those small decisions that become yours at the end of a long marriage. From the window, I can hear the rush of cars on 9th—tires on asphalt reminiscent of waves on shore. I am prone to saying aesthetics matter, and if they do, the moment is beautiful.

I drank my coffee on the futon, quietly, with an air of contemplation. The children sat at the table between the two light-streaming windows, munching cereal. My living room and dining room are one here, the sort of change that only comes about at the end of a long marriage, moving backward in architectural time, traipsing through IKEA, buying a toaster, a dish rack, a set of blue ceramic mugs, using folding chairs as opposed to something solid.

As the light poured in I took photos of the children—my daughter, a peaceful silhouette, lifting spoon toward lips, in the background, a tree's dark limbs, like elongated fingers, and the sun—a spectrum of light—riding in waves behind her. She is never still in life: jumping from couch to couch, performing a play, arguing, putting her little brother in a leg lock. She's as stubborn as stone and willful as a colt. Our days turn into battles of wills reminiscent of Moby Dick and Captain Ahab. I spend swaths of time taking away privileges to maintain a semblance of order, before she rams herself into the raft of our day, smashing it to bits. Her will is so much stronger than mine. Perhaps she is the captain and the whale. Perhaps I am only the boat.

In the second picture, my son runs toward me—shirtless, pale-skinned, red-gold hair shrouded in a halo of the sun's rays that appear as elongated bars chasing him across the room: a gateway into another dimension, a playmate in the world's best game of tag.

The children ignore me at breakfast as I harangue them to finish quickly, to sit while they eat, to stop dropping crumbs on the floor. But now, with two aesthetically pleasing pictures, the banal has been transformed into the beautiful. People love these photos on Instagram. A random person describes my daughter in silhouette as cool. And I hope that this random person on the internet is right because I want to be a photographer and a writer. I want to be something other than what I am: a person who is disappointed with the structure of his life, buzzing from this place to that, from this article about aesthetic theory, to new age philosophy, to a retrospective on modern art, to anything that fills space or suggests an answer to the riddle of living. And it is a riddle, or it always has been for me. What are we to do with the hours that fill our lives?

Art doesn't always mimic life. True mimesis is rare. Those light blooming pictures— aesthetic pleasures—are false. Raising children is not beautiful but banal and tiring. I love them. But I am undone by them: their questions, their inability to buckle seat belts, to sit while they eat, to sleep before 9:30, their insistent fingers pulling arm hair, their bodies—joyful and careless—thrown into my stomach, across my ankles.

    I cannot shit alone. I am undone by their constant need for water, for shows, for candy, for me, for me, for me. How do you make such a chaotic relationship beautiful? How do you make the rote and routine, the tears and the requests to play cars when you don't give two fucks about cars, into something meaningful? Sometimes, I catch myself playing with them at wrestling, growling and tossing them across the floor. I want those moments to last forever, piled beneath blankets, their warm bodies near mine.

I slump into the couch after their bedtime, feeling worn-through around 9:30 or so. Then I can watch a show, read a book, grade a paper, do something that isn't mediated by the necessity of work or parenting. I am impatient with any aspect of life that forces me to conform, to change, to swallow up the selfishness of being me. And I do it, time and time again, I conform, but I am not happy for it.

I'm willing to grant that this questioning of existence is problematic. I act as though some other life exists in which the children wander through waist-high grass chasing butterflies and come in to drink lemonade and hug me before sitting down to discuss the ins and outs of Aristotle's poetics and single-barrel bourbons. I act as though some world exists that was made for my pleasure—long intense chats, slight winds, time stopping amid bluish evening air. That such a world doesn't exist, not for any child, nor any adult, makes it no less disappointing. I cannot manufacture the world I want. As such, I am often disappointed, but I am simultaneously dissatisfied with my dissatisfaction, which I realize is a failure to accept the world as it is, infinitely kinder and gentler than many other people's iterations of the same.

Though perhaps I have it wrong. Perhaps art reminds us that the beautiful has been turned into the banal. Perhaps it's our brains that obscure the beauty around us, furrowing neural pathways designed to make the world easier to comprehend, to perform the rote and routine.

When I think of the world as I see it when I'm taking pictures—light resting in golden hair, the round arch, tattered cloud sky and blooming jacaranda, the soft textures of futons, a spoon's silver sheen—I am reminded that we are surrounded by beauty, by form. Perhaps each day is its own series of beauties—a wind chime near dusk, piles of pink-hued clouds, the lengthening of shadows in the golden hour, an arch, a Doric column, a pansy holding light, a hosta leaf trembling with water, children's pale hands cupping Cheerios, puddles reflecting buildings, clouds, sky. Either argument seems valid to me, beautiful or banal. F. Scott Fitzgerald said, between drinks, "The test of a first-rate intelligence is to hold two opposed ideas in the mind at the same time and still retain the ability to function." I do not have a first-rate mind, but I do have contradictory ideas.

Even if I could trick myself into seeing the light falling sideways across the chaise as gorgeous each morning, my existence would still be problematic. The self still frustrated, incomplete. I don't mean the constructed self, the version we put together each day. Rather, I mean the minute-to-minute self—the self that notices a wine bottle gathering dust, gets up to pee, walks across the house wondering what the bad smell is? Pees, rises and picks up a newspaper article, scans it, puts it down, starts to pour milk into a cereal bowl while thinking of an aunt's Facebook post briefly, before attending to the cracking of eggs, imperfectly. What is that person? Because it seems to me that that is a self, not reflective, not deeply invested in the moment as a continuance of some grand narrative, but passing and passing. All I mean to say is life is not an illumination. It is a series of almost non-contiguous moments. These moments without meaning, in which we exist, in aggregate, compose a self, a life.

I've been reading old essays of mine that I wrote during graduate school, most of which have appeared in one stray place or another. Who knew I'd stopped believing in God at twenty-eight? I always thought the loss had been more recent. In these essays, I repeatedly found passages like the one above, describing life as a series of fragments as opposed to a contiguous whole. Why did I keep writing that time and again? And yet, I also found that I wrote about narrativity, about the stories we tell to structure our lives. It's the writer Joan Didion who says, "We tell ourselves stories in order to live." The saying is too beautiful to disagree with. And I believe the idea that narrative is central to our being has infused my own thoughts, made it a truism though not true. Narrative is a way of stitching things together that might otherwise fall apart: a marriage, a religion. And yet, those stories I told myself about religion and marriage were only half-truths, obscuring the fissures that had been forming for years, moment after moment, decision after decision, change after change. None of which were momentous enough to disrupt the narrative I'd willingly constructed by themselves, but, which in aggregate, were chasm-sized. I realize now that the only story I've ever believed about myself is the story that takes place in the moment, the now. Like every good essayist since Montaigne locked himself away in a French country house to prattle on, I went looking for answers.

It was Borges, as it is for many writers, who led me first. I read his essays a number of years ago. Though I was a different person then, still married, still somewhat content with the structures of life, sitting on a beige couch, poring over his essays and stories on evenings when the first child, then a baby, was asleep. She was pink and cream-colored. She laughed when I made sounds like a bird. I am no longer that man as I sit on a futon, two blocks from that house, in a single bedroom apartment, typing in the late evening on a warm summer's day. But I digress, as I often do. In his essay, "The Nothingness of Personality," Borges says, "There is no whole self…I, as I write this, am only a certainty that seeks out the words that are most apt to compel your attention. That proposition and few muscular sensations, and the sight of limpid branches that the trees place outside my window constitute my current I." The limpid branches, the fingers framing my daughter's silhouette. Indeed, say I, the self is an absence, and now it is I, the self of this moment, who tries to find the words to compel you.

Descartes says, "I think therefore I am." But what if I am not what I think? God says, "I am the great I am." Ergo, I am because I am. The latter construction gives me a glimmer of hope because my thoughts have always been elliptic, contingent, a raft in the tempest of the day.

But what person has intellectualized themselves into happiness? What person has gained an answer by cataloging their inconsistencies, foibles, the mind's wild meander? What existentialist philosopher has promised a happy life? Nietzsche: "The thought of suicide is a great consolation: by means of it one gets through many a dark night." I sought solace in religion instead. Years ago, I'd practiced meditation during a tumultuous period in my life. Like most westerners now, I figured I'd try Buddhism light.

The next morning, I tried to calm my thoughts while sitting in the backyard of my former house. The yard was encircled by a wooden fence I'd once priced out with various contractors—a task that fell to me as means of getting some autonomy in our marriage. She and I agreed that I did not do enough, though we disagreed on the reason why. On the borders of the fence lay blackberries, red and unripe, small white-blossomed flowers, purple coneflowers, down-turned petals like the ears of a wet dog, Black-eyed Susan's pressing into patches of weed stricken grass, clover, an old stump that turns up mushrooms each June.

As I sat on the grey porch steps, I narrowed my focus—a green-backed fly rubbed his feelers together on the bench in front of me, two gnats, ghosted in and out of sight depending on the slant of light, an ant crawled on a blade of grass. I took it all in—felt slightly more at peace with myself—no oneness of being, but a small shelter. But the pursuit of transcendence is in the intellectual air these days and as easy to take up as to put down. And the day, as it always does, held so many other things.

The British philosopher, Galen Strawson, wrote a paper called *Against Narrativity*. In the paper, Strawson claims that the popular conception of the self is narrative in nature, which relies on a story that we tell ourselves about our lives. This view is shared by the philosopher Daniel Dennett and the scientist Oliver Sacks. However, Strawson, a philosopher at the University of Reading, posits that we don't all tell stories to construct our lives. He describes a second way of being a person in the world as episodic. Strawson describes the difference thusly, "one naturally figures oneself, considered as a self, as something that was there in the (further) past and will be there in the (further) future. If one is episodic, one does not figure oneself, considered as a self, as something that was there in the (further) past and will be there in the (further) future."

I am an unreliable narrator of my own life. It has the ring of truth. Often, looking at my past self is the same as peering through a glass darkly. I recognize the actors, but I can't place them in relation to the self of now. As a result, I often find relationships, even long-term ones, very dependent on the moment, on a particular interaction, bad or good, and I extrapolate that interaction out over the whole course of that relationship, so tied to the moment, conceiving a near eternity from a fraction, easily in love, easily out of love.

As I wrote that first morning, a fly buzzed in dizzying circles over the smoky dark glass of craft beer, over Bib and Tucker's amber whiskey bottle, a gift from my now separated in-laws. The fly sailed past the small, brooding statues of Rodin's *The Thinker*. I once saw the full statue of *The Thinker* in Paris with my former in-laws. It was raining that day, a low grey sky, and as I stood in the garden, contemplating that massive statue, tears seemed to gather round his eyes, fell dramatically off his nose. And all that's left now are the moments and it is up to me to revise them, to make meaning of things now passed.

Here is what I remember most about that day spent looking at Rodin's statues: not his statues, but those of his lover, Camille Claudel. In her sculptures, two bodies are torn from one another, a lover walks away while his counterpart cries on the floor. She begs to be seen by him, to be held. After the separation, my mother said, to be fully known and not loved, is the worst thing in the world. I don't know if a work of art has ever left me so viscerally sad as Claudel's sculptures.

I used to lie awake as a child, scared for hours by every creak, imagining my impending death. I am certain I will be murdered. I am certain I will die on a flight. I am certain I will be eaten by a bear. I hope that a bear doesn't eat me on a plane. My son hasn't murdered me yet though. He climbs into bed and pinwheels round, a ball of kinetic sleep energy, raising hell—jabbing ribs, stealing covers, sweating profusely. I sleep like hell when he sneaks into bed. In the morning, I wrap my arms around him and squeeze his warm body. I already miss these days that have not passed.

My son asked me, as the fly careered around the room, just what flies want. He has a fuzzy mop of golden-red hair, is kind, and taken to stories with no real point, movement, or discernable end, a born essayist. He interrupts himself mid-story when something else crosses his field of vision, and the stories often end in dismemberment, punching, and dragons.

"It looks for things to eat," I said of the fly.

"They like burgers," my son observed, surveying the small store of information he had on houseflies.

"Yes," I said. "They like burgers."

The fly circled the small orange vacuum cleaner and landed on a puzzle piece displaying a leopard's paw. We'd constructed the puzzle months ago, something I brought over in the early days of the separation when I was trying to create a new and happy life, setting new patterns, new ways to stitch our lives together.

Life has repetitions, morning routines, commutes, jobs, teeth brushing, vacuuming the floor, but most of life lacks meaning. I suspect that my frustration with the world has to do with this meaning-making faculty, which is constantly frustrated by the reality of a disorganized, meaningless world. You brush your teeth to keep away cavities, weed the garden to allow flowers to grow, pull leaves from the gutter to avoid clogging the downspout, have the water heater and furnace checked yearly, and on and on and on, but what is it all for? My brain throbs in the background. What is it all for? Is this the thing? Is this?

Socrates said that man learned by being in discussion daily about excellence. I am daily in a discussion about the quality of baked goods and whether the milk tastes sour. I am in discussions of snap peas, of renewing library books, of complaining how tired we all are.

The fly doesn't seem to have any pattern. Sometimes it brushes the window, at others, it hovers near the edge of the futon, given to me by my sister-in-law and her husband when they learned I was moving out.

I live alone now, at least part-time. The kids spend every Tuesday and Wednesday with me and every other weekend. We laugh and read books, but mostly we argue—over bath time, over broccoli eating, scooter usage, screen time. Sometimes I shout at them when they come out of their room at night and it's past nine o'clock. "Daddy has this paper to grade!" Or, "Daddy needs some time to do adult things. It's too late. Go to bed. You guys drive me crazy." I hope that they forget so many nights.

My daughter is a hellion but so quiet in her sleep. Come morning, I like to wake her up softly, slowly, rubbing her shoulder in sleep. "Good morning, love," I say to her as she swims up from dreams. She knows how to be good, but she is only interested when it intersects with her desires. In this way, she and I are alike.

Am I unhappy? Aren't we all? Don't we paper over it with nice cars, French doors, new drapes, pictures of our trips to the lake, turning over the garden, researching breakfast sandwich places, prestige television shows, house plants, travels to Europe? Of course, my papering is that of middle-class privilege. I suspect that other people house their unhappiness in different places. Perhaps I should be more resistant to confusing my life and unhappiness with everyone else's. I think I might be unhappy, but I can't be sure. In fact, I'm rarely sure of anything, especially myself.

I listen to music as I drive the children to school, trying to assuage the light feeling of dread, of having been there before, driven this same route, listened to these same songs, had these same tired thoughts about my life. How should I live? How should I live? How should I live? The music drowns out the children, who are always grasping for my attention. Other days, I feel guilty. I turn the music down and ask them to tell me about their lives. The girl asks questions about birthday parties or describes, in rich details, the trials and travails of characters in *Everafter High*. She reminds me of a promise to watch *Sofia the First*, of a particularly good dessert she once had with friends. The boy rambles about trucks that turn into dinosaurs and then the story pivots into something about bones and a new friend. He's a post-modernist, my boy.

He may be a genius. He understands that everything has meaning.

Nothing seems to belong in my life. The clouds have taken over now, but I can still see the green leaves of the sage and rosemary, chlorophyll gleaming in the half-light. I used to garden at the house we shared, planted seed after seed, made a row of peas that sent their tendrils off in search of sky. Before getting into the car, the children and I would pick snap peas from the vines, delighted to find so many. "Daddy, I see one." Now, that same space is full of weeds and a few stray poppies that waited a year to appear.

The children want me to play, to ride swings, to build tracks, to watch them on a slide, on a tractor. But I am tired, and I lie on the wooden bench at the park and read essays about the work of Joy Williams, of A.O. Scott, of David Foster Wallace. Finally, after putting them off for hours, I half-heartedly join the children at play, climbing onto rocks, onto playground equipment, lying in the grass with them, skin itching. I help build an imaginary cake and pretend to be Thunder, a pliant dog. I do all of this in a tired state, half-aware at best, as I often am with the children. And yet, I know that my wild independent streak, not always immediately apparent because I am easy-going and a people pleaser, causes me to rebel in these moments, to operate in them with a kind of post-Thanksgiving torpor. I act as if my children were not living their lives, their joyous, ridiculous little lives, while I sat on a bench reading. Briefly, I watched two varieties of bumblebees pollinating the swaying bits of white clover, bee's bodies curling around the head of a flower as if it were a lover being pulled in for a kiss. Then I'm asked to be back in the game, patrolling a spare bit of aluminum bench, bored shitless.

It's in these moments when I'm wishing time away, that I suspect other people's interior lives must be different than my own. I cannot imagine that everyone experiences such profound boredom when they are tasked with watching the children. I experience much of my life as boring. I crave novelty as other people crave alcohol. Although I don't know if it's a feature of my interior life that causes this discomfort with daily life, or whether everyone else has encountered that same boredom and pushed beyond it into the realm of meaning. I'd spent the prior day with a lovely couple, parents of three. The wife kept them busy with the pool, with lunch, with chalk, and she talked and talked of the things she'd bought for the children, the way she'd kept them entertained, prattling for hours, happy to watch and talk of the children. In an idle moment, she talked of returning to work, then said, "Its been a good seven years but also mind-numbing."

The four-year-old proposed a fly swatter, but I tell him I haven't got one. He's tired of being buzzed by the fly, but I'm fine. Why carve away at the narrow hollow of life that this housefly has? It'll be gone soon enough. Twenty-eight days, that's it. No need to swat at its thin tendril of life. A recent study in the Proceedings of the National Academy of Sciences suggests that insects do have the rudiments of consciousness, a mid-brain, and subjective experience, i.e., it feels like something to be a fly, maybe. The study concludes that, like humans, flies are egocentric.

Before the separation, my mother noted that I am a bit self-involved.

I feel my children are slipping away from me. I read that by age twelve you'll have already spent half the time you will ever get in your child's life. Do I have the right to miss children that I've freely chosen to leave for half the week? This is the double bind of being a parent. I miss them terribly, and when I'm with them, I find them difficult, needy. I often can't wait to be away from them. This ambivalence is at the core of what I'm feeling. I don't want to miss out on their childhood, but I often find myself missing out on it anyway.

I like mornings because my desire for other people is dimmed. I spend evenings reading articles, chatting lightly with friends, eager for people to validate my existence in the world by acknowledging that I am an interesting and fun human being. This desire for affirmation, for conversation, for some connection, rests overnight, and I wake up, shower and eat breakfast, without feeling the press of need for other people, which rises as the day goes on. Often this press goes unmet, and I read, restlessly, quickly. I don't know why I crave other people so deeply. Or perhaps I do. Perhaps in writing this essay I've managed to stumble upon something. I crave novelty, love travel, new bakeries, wines. Repetition, as I told a friend in a bar last night, repetition kills me. What I find in conversation, in an e-mail, in contact with other human beings, at least the interesting ones, is a temporary respite from that repetition, a suggestion that life isn't all the same rote forms day after day, month after month. Or perhaps it's a manifestation of my core episodic nature, constantly reliant upon a moment to find meaning. Thus, if the moments are repetitious, dull, drab, then meaning must not exist.

I should like to think that this desire, thirst, or craving, is some attendant feature of modern life, representative of a culture that focuses on the nuclear family, on cell phones and messaging over face to face communication, that prioritizes work and productivity. And yet, Schopenhauer wrote about the twin poles of boredom and desire, and the Buddha, 2,500 years ago, wrote about the monkey mind and the sorrows of life. There is nothing new under the sun.

The fly died this afternoon. My son noticed its body first, resting limply in the sill. The fly had buzzed about for its allotted time, and now I could let it sleep in peace. The project had been absurd, had resulted in the children asking me if flies liked cornbread, if flies stung, if flies belonged in our house or outside, and many more fly-related questions, which I've since forgotten. What purpose was served by letting that myopic and self-centered fly live out its days? I used to believe in God, His hand, ready to smash my body against the screen of the universe.

But I don't believe in God. I believe in peace, so I let the fly live. Just tonight, my son grew upset when I squished a bug on the kitchen floor. "That could be a mommy or a daddy," he said.

All I want is this sort of peace that I sometimes find in moments, extended out for a very long period of time. All I want is so many things.

My children are four and six. We've spent the last three weeks watching a fly bump against the window in the capital of the United States while the President is tweeting, scant miles away, about the appearance of a television host. My wife and I have been texting about whether the impending divorce will hurt our children's chances of being well-adjusted humans. I submit to her that no one is well-adjusted. All those religious folks we'd grown up with, taking pictures of their happy white suburban lives, now seem like delusional fools.

In the evening, I get coffee with an old friend I've lost track of, and we chat for a while. This friend tells me they thought briefly of suicide, of ending the charade of life. And though I'm never quite satisfied, it is that desire or hope that one day I will be that pulls me along like a stick in the current of a river, like a human in the river of time.

When I got home that evening, the house was swarming with flies. Five of them soared up from the chaise and made dizzying circles. Three were attached to one window, four to the other. That single fly had laid eggs in the trash and the larvae had come of age, an explosion. The house smelled like death. Everywhere I went, I saw flies, lifting from the wall, circling the stove, bumping into my leg, my arms. I swatted one on the bathroom mirror, then smashed wildly at my face as I tried to pee without being landed on.

    I slept poorly, thinking of flies landing on me in the dark. It's the day my soon-to-be-ex and I are celebrating Father's Day. I celebrate by battling flies. There is no ritual bathing, no Agamemnon sacrificing his child, no building of horses or driving of bodies behind chariots. It was a slaughter. After a few tepid swipes with a newspaper, I realized my flip flops were the best weapon. And though I felt my skin crawling, I started to smash flies as though I were born to it. I have quick hands and good coordination. I pirouetted, swinging my arm like a scythe to wheat, bringing death from above. I was radiant with it. A fly landed above the stove, and I swung quickly, it moved at the last second, but I managed to twist around and catch it mid-flight, backhanding it across the room where it squirmed until I smashed it. I moved through the house like a panther, menacing flies, swinging my sandal like a mace, catching flies unaware, sitting on windows, on walls, unsuspecting. I tried to drown a pair in the sink. I swatted one in the bathroom who fell straight into the trash can. I crushed them, balletically.

Did you know that flies sometimes play dead? It's something I didn't realize until that day. In Woolf's essay, "The Death of a Moth," she says as she watches the moth die, that the desire is all on the side of the living, but I've just crushed a moth on my sandal, my sentiments, being decidedly with that of the sandal and death, but I have no corollary war as Woolf did in WWII, or if I do, it is happening across oceans, far out of sight, out of mind, a symptom of my own twenty-first century capitalistic myopia about death from above.

On the way home from Father's Day breakfast, she and I talk about how having a new relationship might affect the children, talk of who is in charge, whether those new people would be allowed to be jealous. The thing is, and some person might tell you this is just a narrative trope and feature of post-modernism, but we are better apart. In fact, I'm best apart. I make a good friend and a damn near fantastic date. What follows, I make messes of.

I've been listening to therapy podcasts about marriage, couples who have consented to have their sessions recorded and aired. As a listener, it's easy to diagnose other people's issues. The therapist, a straight-talking Canadian, stops the husband from talking, noting that he tends to make everything about himself. It's a habit that my spouse and I were both guilty of during the long year when we lived together before the separation, but I couldn't see it then. The self, narcissistic as a fly, silly and emotional as a child, obscures the very world that it seeks to comprehend.

I listened to a second podcast, *On Being*, when the interviewer talked to the pop philosopher, Alain De Botton, about the unrealistic expectations we put on our romantic relationships. De Botton points out that our attitude and expectations about marriage have shifted over time: at first, we expected babies, then property, then security, now, we wanted all those things coupled with romantic love. As he notes, it's a bit much. I've lived the majority of my life, fourteen or so on, waiting for external love or experience to fill my inner need for contentment.

And though I recognize that no experience or relationship can solve the problem of how to live, I cannot deny its allure. In fact, during the first two or three dates, weeks, months, and sometimes years, a relationship, dopamine-filled, can feel like it will never slow down, never recede. Even something as small as a good conversation can sometimes send me spinning into externalities, possible futures, walks on city streets at night, trampling leaves. I cannot see the end of those days, which is the only certainty. Self-knowledge is not always useful.

I am sitting on the futon again while clouds pile up in the distance like bits of cream, barely moving on the blued horizon. A fly struggles against the window, suffocating between panes of glass, and I am content to watch it meander across this tableaux, watch it dive bomb to the bottom in hopes of escape.

Just as I've ended the essay, a fly lands on top of the computer screen, thick, black, ugly. Make meaning of that, make meaning of that.

Weeks later, I open the trash can and a Biblical pestilence of flies pours fourth, black bodies filling my vision, their dull hum, forcing me to bend backward and begin retreating from that awful horde. And then, for a brief moment, they stopped flying, and I was able to make sense of the scene, a white trash bag, hundreds of flies nesting in the basin of the can. I tossed the trash in and slammed the top shut.

I walked up the steps and inside the empty house, just the outlines of where the children had slept the night before, empty bunk beds, empty pillows, you fill in the rest.

You can look for meaning all your life, but perhaps it's only of your own devising.

Perhaps you only find meaning when walking around the house, sandal in hand, bringing death from above. Why end there? On the flies and emptiness. Reader, haven't you been paying attention? There is no deeper or hidden meaning, just the moment, a hundred buzzing flies, whirring by like words on a screen, passing and passing, like moments, like days, like lives.

Home Burial

Long before I had children of my own, I fell in love with the poem, "Home Burial," by Robert Frost. I'm not sure why "Home Burial," a poem about marriage and children, made such an impact on a college student, much more than two roads diverging in a wood, which is practically an inspiration poster for the life everyone is shooting for in college. And yet, I have always been interested in the drama of human relations, in what causes fusion, in what causes breakage. There was something beautiful about the sadness in "Home Burial."

In the Frost poem, a young farmer and his wife struggle in the aftermath of a child's death. The farmer, ferocious with pain, quickly digs a hole in the yard, gravel flying behind him. His wife, a city person, watches in horror, mistaking his sad fury as ruthless efficiency. Once inside, the farmer, the gravel still fresh on his feet, mumbles that even the finest birch can be rotted by three day's fog. The wife reproaches the husband for thinking of farming even on the day their child has died.

I've read that the death of a child is the most psychologically damaging event that can happen in a person's life. Certainly, this is context-dependent as we now expect children to live out their full stretch of days. Nearly two decades after I first read that poem, I have two children of my own, who fly around my apartment with such wild abandon that I can see how losing them would unmake me, so radically have they altered the shape of my days, the contours of my self. It is possible to change spouses, change jobs, to dream of other people, funnier, more forgiving with the finances, or a house with better pipes, a bay window. But I never daydream of other children. I'm happily stuck with my two, even through their obstinacy and fighting. Just this evening, I knocked my daughter's head against the bed by accident as I pulled her away from her brother. I'll hate you forever, she said. But forever is a long time, and we were reading *The Secret Garden* in a matter of minutes.

We don't bury our dead in the yard anymore. No symmetrical line of gravestones beneath the sycamore to remind us of life's definitive end. No running of fingers along the limestone, tracing the years of the lives that have come before our own.

The Neanderthals, Homo sapiens oft-parodied cousins, buried their dead. The earliest known burial site is from 50,000 years ago at a cave in southwestern France. Initially, there was a dispute in the scientific community about whether the body had been intentionally buried or not. There is a tendency to ascribe non-human characteristics to the Neanderthals, which helps protect our conception of humans as a special chain on the link of evolution. And perhaps we are, but the Neanderthals buried their dead, wore jewelry, and painted the walls of caves. In Shanidar cave in Iraq, one of the skeletons had pollen on it, suggesting that the burial site had been covered with flowers. Certainly, consciousness must have resided there, what a religious person might call a soul.

We know so little about the lives that are not our own. Our view of life is but a sliver of light in the thick velvety darkness. This is not a novel statement, but death brings the limits of our knowledge into sharp focus. What do we really know about Neanderthals or a great aunt? Remember that any summary of life, even a well-written biography, fails to capture the details that comprise a life: the quiet evenings by the sink, the way a person smiled or laughed, an April sunset turning crimson behind a row of beech that sets them into a reverie of childhood, which is itself, misremembered, since accessing a memory changes its form.

But in truth, we don't always want to know more. In fact, I think we've banished death to the outskirts of our lives, so we can imagine ourselves deathless. Not immortal, mind you, just absent death. We know that it will come for all of us, but it's an abstraction, as opposed to a reality. I suspect that it comforts us to keep death safely tucked away. And we lose something that humans have often had, a reminder that our lives are parabolic, and need to be given shape. In confronting death, we realize how little we know about the lives of others, and by extension, how little we know about our own. In death's absence, we can continue to putter around, content in our delusion that the ride is never going to end, that we've always got another turn around the room. Our lives are an enigma, lived but not comprehended.

My grandparents bought two burial plots near Sebastopol, California. Sebastopol is a small town, nestled in a small valley near the endless green hillocks of wine country. The sunlight falls nearly every day there—on the dusty boughs of apple trees and on the hillsides checkered by vines. If my parents had stayed together, I would have grown up in Sebastopol. When they parted, the land where I was to have grown up was sold, and I only visited relatives there every now and again. We'd drive on the winding roads, up gravel paths, past vineyards and big houses with acres and acres of yard. From there, I could briefly glimpse a life that could have been my own.

My grandmother lived in Sebastopol for most of her adult

life, including the thirty-nine years after her husband died. As a child, my father used to drive us from San Jose to Sebastopol on roads dense with Eucalyptus, so famous now for the way they burst during wildfires. Once, on a long car ride, I remember staring at the sun until I felt I could see its surface, everything was a roiling purple and my eyes were filled with wavering spots for hours after.

When we arrived, grandmother, who was just a shade under five feet, would greet us all with a hug and a firm and distinctive peck on each cheek. She always seemed to be on the verge of laughter, and her cheeks were deep, round and red. She was also quick to diffuse the tension my father seemed intent on creating in his idle hassling of us. Oh, John, she'd say, cut it out. I suspect that my father was bored and perhaps displeased with his lot in life, which I'm not sure he gave any deep thought to, or made any attempt to change.

Grandmother's husband, Julian, the name I gave my son, died of a brain tumor ten years before I was born. Often, Julian was spoken of in glowing terms. Hagiography is often wedded to early deaths. It's about the only reason I'd want to go early, so everyone would remember me fondly and not as the inconsistent and sometimes troubled human I am. I know next to nothing about Julian, save that he enjoyed working on cars. And thus, I know nothing about how he related to my own father, who was bereft at his sudden death. And by extension, what role their relationship played in my father's relationship to us, which was haphazard, childish, and occasionally shot through with kindness.

After we'd been hugged, grandma hustled us into the kitchen, where she served us apple juice and salami. The juice was served in small glass cups that I now have in my small apartment.

Painted on the glasses are scenes from cities across the world: Paris, Havana, Hague, Madrid—all the places I want to someday go. My grandmother's house had wind chimes hung from the rafters of her porch, and a large kitchen window that looked out over a small, rocky garden. There was a clothes line in the center of the yard such as you used to see in the last century and lines of thick green moss grew between the spaces of a red brick path. Whenever I hear the tinkling of wind chimes, even now, decades later, I think of my grandmother's house, and by extension, childhood, and the days there, which were sweet, short and strange. Back then, my mind was still busy in a way that it rarely is now, registering the wind chimes, the folds of my grandmother's face, the slight turn in my father's voice when he thought we should be doing more to help his mother.

I learned to play card games in her house, lengthy games of war that I sometimes played on my own, and Go Fish. At night, I slept in an oak sleigh bed, which had belonged to her parents when they first immigrated from Italy to San Francisco. From bed, I'd stare up at the popcorn ceiling, afraid of the dark and of the picture of my nana and papa. They glared at the camera and their clothes seemed like they were from centuries before. They looked like ghosts. And yet, all I have is this image of Nona and Papa, not even a story or two about them to round it out. Were they stern or quick to laugh like my grandmother? What was their day-to-day life like in Italy? My relatives are merely a severe-looking picture on a wall, no more realized than a fly that buzzed around my apartment for a week last summer and about whom I'd written an elliptical essay. The real memory of those nights is that I wet the bed until I was eight, waking up each morning in a small circle of pee, pajamas wet. And my father would come in and strip the sheets, and I'd change into my clothes for the day, ashamed.

My children are now five and seven, and each month or two seems to bring a new change in their lives, and I am forced to adapt, to reconceive of them on the fly. The other day, as I drove down the busy streets of Washington, D.C., which branch like tributaries toward home, my daughter said that one of my son's friends was going to buy him a present. My son interjected, You can't know what someone else is thinking. You can't get in anyone else's brain. I've been having trouble writing fiction these last two years, something I'd done almost exclusively during my graduate program in creative writing. But now, I find myself locked in my own mind, only able to attend to the drumbeat of my own thoughts.

I do not know the ins and outs of my grandmother's days, whether she went to the grocery store on Wednesday or visited her younger sister, Marie, who lived on a hillside apple farm, on the weekends. When she died, my grandmother chose not to be buried in the plot she'd bought with Julian, her spouse of thirty-two years, who was, by all hagiographic accounts, a good man. Instead, she was cremated, and we spread her ashes in the Sierra Nevada mountains, a thick line of granite, rising thousands of feet—the backbone of northern California. I do not know why she wasn't buried with Julian. The secret of their lives, of her decision, is now between her and the mountains.

The Egyptians were some of the first to bury their dead. The burial practice began as shallow graves, the kind which now call serial killers to mind. However, their burial rites grew into more elaborate practices—a mastaba was used by royal families and the upper class alike. The mastaba was a rectangular brick building with inward sloping sides. Inside, the dead were buried with jewelry, weapons, and food, which helped to guide the deceased on the journey into the afterlife.

My daughter has a small piece of fabric that she calls Yaya. She's had the small piece of fabric since the day she was born. We have pictures of Yaya, a rectangle of pink with a small satin face and arms, cradled in her fleshy arms. My daughter is now seven and still thinks that Yaya is alive. Before she leaves her mother's house, she tucks Yaya into bed and lets her know when she'll be back. The other night, she had a mental breakdown asking whether life would just end at death, wondering if Yaya would accompany her to heaven. I told her about the Egyptians then, promised that someone would bury her with Yaya, so she could accompany her to the afterlife. My daughter said, But if I die and don't remember anything, life will have been worthless. I said, If you die and don't remember anything, it won't matter. You won't remember it. As she bawled, something inside me softened. I ran my hand across her wet cheeks. I reminded her about heaven, which I don't believe in.

I have no jewelry to be interred with, but I'd like to be interred with my iPhone, so I can keep posting pictures from the other side of death. From death, I'll post pictures of the River Styx, of Uggulino consuming his children, of the velvety darkness that will encompass me, stretching on endlessly in both directions, like the dark matter that holds together the universe.

A decade ago, my former wife and I traveled to Italy and hiked in the Cinque Terre region of Italy. The five towns, comprised of brightly colored houses, are strewn like diamonds across the thin ravines that briefly flatten out before pouring into the Ligurian

Sea. We walked between the five towns on a dusty trail, with the sea gleaming like the back of a serpent below. Just above Vernazza, where we were staying, was a cemetery, where large and ornate above-ground tombs lined the top of the hillside. We walked amongst the graves, fading flowers, marble columns. The sky was a warm blue and a low layer of thin clouds made little impact on the light. We couldn't tell if everyone at the grave was a tourist, or whether some of the people might have been locals visiting grandmothers, uncles, mothers and fathers.

It was Napoleon, who first declared that the graves must be outside of town for health reasons. And so they'd been moved to the top of the hillside where the dead now have the best view of cliffs and sea. The cemetery is now closed to visitors, who, like us, overused it to death.

Most cemeteries encourage you to buy your plot or crypt before you die. When you purchase a plot, you have interment rights. Simply put, the right to have your body buried there. Interestingly, if someone changes their mind about the burial, the cemetery must be offered those interment rights before they are offered to another individual. However, the cemetery can refuse to buy back those interment rights, which means, I suppose, that you could sell that plot to the highest bidder. I do not know who lies in the grave next to my grandfather, or whether he is lonely in the afterlife.

I haven't visited a grave in years now. I don't know if it's because the graves of loved ones are so far away or because I don't care much about the dead, what they might have to tell me. What would I learn about my own life by contemplating death via something physical as opposed to abstract? My life is primarily comprised of abstractions, scattered thoughts. However, to be fair to myself, I read a good deal. And many of the authors I read are now dead, and I'm carrying on a conversation with them now. Just the other day, I checked out *The Tibetan Book of Living and Dying*. I doubt I'll read it, but it's a nice book to have on the shelf, reminding myself that I could theoretically contemplate the end.

Oscar Wilde: "Death happens only once, but for such a very long time."

Some Native American tribes buried their dead in the trees. The corpse was wrapped in a blanket and placed in a spot where branches came together or near the top, where the multitude of branches could hold the weight of the body. Sometimes belongings were also hung in the tree, one more reminder of life. What it would be like to come upon one of those graves, the wind blowing through, stirring the leaves, a blanket, and the tattered remains of a body. It strikes me as macabre. But, of course, it's just a different burial practice. There is nothing inherently macabre about hanging a body in a tree, more than there is something macabre about burying them in the ground or burying them in the mastaba. Some mornings, their tree must be full of bird song, and imagine your bleached bones filled with morning light and song.

The morning we spread my grandmother's ashes, we stood in a circle, my mother, my father, myself, my former wife, along with two aunts and an uncle. A family. I don't entirely remember what we said about Margaret Springer. I'm giving her maiden name back to her now, as she gave herself the freedom to be buried alone. We must have said kind things, good things, for she was a kind and good woman. At least as I knew her, the sliver of her made available to me. I emptied a portion of the urn, shocked at how the ashes just kept pouring, too heavy for the breeze. Grandmother was being poured onto the unwelcome granite, where later she'd be washed away by rain. She had always been extraordinarily kind. I can still hear her small trill of laughter. She laughed like a wind chime.

It's hard not to think of my own religious upbringing and the burial of the first son, Christ. In that story, death is merely the beginning of our much longer eternal lives. As a child and into my teenage years, I used to sit in bed and contemplate eternity, time-stretching forever before me. The thought terrified me. The idea of time without end is conceptually antithetical to the way that I experience life, moment to moment, breath to breath.

There is a downloadable app, *We Croak*, which reminds you five times a day that you're going to die. This slight chirp and reminder surprise me, not because it bridges the gap between our lives and their finite nature, but rather, it strikes me as a testament to the staggering reality that everything will be mechanized and monetized.

Some tribes in Africa carry the dead out through a hole in the wall, so they cannot find their way back home. Others zig-zag on the way to the burial site, in an attempt to ward off the same. Others are buried at home, the family eager to welcome them back in their new shape in the afterlife. I wonder where Julian would have been buried had he lived in Africa. My grandmother would have been buried close to home.

The truth is, I don't much care for being reminded of my insignificance, even if it's technically true; it sours the occasion of life, which I sour enough on my own.

The other night, my son launched into a fit of crying as we lay together in the dark, body wracked by sobs. He said, I don't want to die, daddy, wrenching the words out from his insides time and time again, a small child, terrified. I tried what I could to help, reminding him that everyone had to die. I often try and be scrupulously honest with the children because I suspect their mother of sugar-coating things. After ten minutes of crying, I told him he and I would live for a very, very long time. Eventually, he started to settle down. I'd explained to him that many people are turned into ash after death. And he said that he could keep my pile of ashes next to his bed when he grew up, so he could roll over and snuggle me whenever he wanted. Yes, I said, that's a great idea.

Epicurus believed in the gods, but he thought that they were so far beyond humans that it was useless to pay them any mind. He also taught his followers to think of death as a constant, a reality for everyone, which meant that you should also spend little time on it. By having death constantly in front of you, you could fully embrace life. His teachings, the finest I'd encountered in my newly secular life, focused on gardening, drinking, thinking, and sex.

Sometimes if you look through the kaleidoscope of days you'll begin to see a pattern that wasn't immediately obvious. My daughter and I were driving home from her school, summer was just beginning and the azaleas were in late bloom, an array of color—bright pink, red, violet, blue. The drive home from school is short but packed with cars, other people navigating the small roads that cross over the long stretch of Washington, D.C. taken up by the Old Soldier's Home. We were talking about car accidents, and my son asked how many people died in car accidents. A lot, I said. How many? he countered. Lots, I said. Because children are forever asking questions for which I do not know the answer. We'll look it up later, I told him.

Just then, my daughter piped in. Dad, she said, if I die soon I'd like my ashes to be put beneath the maple tree at mommy's house. The tree had been planted the year my daughter was born. I watched as a crew of men quickly transformed the square plot of grass into a pollinator garden, rife with coneflowers, Black-eyed Susan's, yarrow. Then, that afternoon, while I watched from the window of what was to have been my writing study, the oak in the alley shed bit after bit of yellow-green pollen, fat, caterpillar like shapes, coating the newly made yard in something that made it appear sickly, overrun.

In Buddhism, I read that I'm supposed to let go of my attachment to the world. Only then, will life begin to have meaning and death will make sense. But what if I want to cling to the world: to treasure the warmth of the children, to treasure the way that red wine makes me feel so fearless, to treasure the sunlight lying in the rust-colored leaves of an oak, to treasure the way bodies curl together after sex, spent and satisfied.

In the car, while my daughter spoke calmly about where she'd like her ashes spread, I wanted to cry. She is so new to this bright and terrible world. And though I can see that it sometimes will be a mess for her wildly intense emotions and fierce desire to be seen, still, she too will cling to this world. I do not cry in front of the children though. I keep it inside. My tears are saved up for times when I am alone. Instead, I told my daughter that I'd rather she was buried in the side yard.

HOME BURIAL

Her mother and I had worked very hard on that yard two years after we'd moved into the house. We pulled out the grass, laid down a drop cloth, choking off the weeds, spread a layer of dirt and then layer after layer of gravel. Then we set down flagstones for a path. It was precisely the sort of project I'd done for my mother in my own youth. As the years passed in our side yard and my wife and I grew apart, I planted woodland phlox, columbines, ferns, hostas, coral honeysuckle that snakes up the cable wire and blooms against a backdrop of blue sky, a cardinal climber that is growing bushy along the fence, pink and purple tulips, small creeping flowers that carpet the ground in green and burst forth in purple come spring. Who knew that the garden would last longer than the marriage?

There are only stones over there daddy, my daughter said. I'd get blown all over the yard. Yes, I answered, I guess you would. And you wouldn't want to be thrown around the yard, snagged on a tree's branches, or mashed into the underside of the fence, would you? Couldn't you just bury me under the maple tree if I die? she asked. It was a sensible request from my child. I almost laughed; this wild and wonderful child, this silly and sad life.

The Leopard

A leopard can't change its spots. When I read to my children, then very young, their warm bodies curled against me on the couch, they loved to hear the violent animal noises I made when I read *Polar Bear, Polar Bear, What Do You Hear?* As I read, the introduction of each animal was accompanied by the most realistic noise I could muster—the trumpet of an elephant, the yelp of a peacock, growl of a bear. I went so far as to research the correct sounding noises online, making sure my trumpets and growls approximated nature. My best was the guttural snarl I made for the leopard, deep and concussive, a snarl that often left me coughing for minutes after. Elephant, Elephant, what do you hear? I hear a leopard snarling in my ear. The children laughed in delight, and asked to hear the sounds again and again.

Times change. The pattern of light moves from spring to summer and birds migrate through the cathedral of sky, caterpillars change shape, become butterflies. I no longer read the children books on that couch. My ex-wife and I separated, and I moved out. Now I live blocks away, and they are getting a bit too old to appreciate a guttural snarl. Instead, we read about wizards and wardrobes in this little life I continue to cobble together in my apartment, with its small succulents, abundant bookshelves, pictures of monasteries on greenish waters, the Alhambra, Lake Bled, cities I've traveled through since I left home. All the invisible cities of dreams, being made visible.

THE BODY IS A TEMPORARY GATHERING PLACE

*

In the early stages of the pandemic, on the heels of a breakup with a long-term girlfriend, a relationship I thought might last forever, one that might reify my mistake of having not made the marriage work, I walked the streets in my neighborhood in a fixed pattern. First, I walked the numerical streets, which cut horizontally through the small Brightwood subdivision in Washington, D.C., where my apartment and former house are, blocks away from my ex-wife, so we could easily walk the children back and forth to one another—duplexes mostly, some single-family homes, scattered chain-link fences, scrambling squirrels, towering oaks lining the streets, or smaller ginkgo. On my walks, I passed a community garden I'd always intended to get a plot in. The garden was flanked by a large green field where starlings sifted the ground for worms, small beaks darting into the soil. As I walked, I cried, and I sifted my own life for some sense of meaning, of what went wrong between the dreams of adulthood and the adult ashes of my life, answers that must lie, squirming beneath the surface and roiling emotions.

I'd lived a typical life, had two children, bought a house, but a strange undercurrent of dissatisfaction with something had always been present, and then my life turned as topsy-turvy as a wild stream, emboldened by spring rain. Suddenly, the choice of what I was to be felt open again, as opposed to determined. Thus, the spring walks, the crisp air, the scattering birds and pale blue skies, were all reminders of my essential and startling solitude. I'd see a house my girlfriend and I would have once sent to each other via text: faded bricks, roses climbing a trellis, a quiet sunroom, windows over the garden, suddenly blurring, fading, pictures unsent, lives unlived.

On other days, the children are a hum of activity, fights on Zoom calls, distracted calls of "Dad, Dad, Dad" at every moment. Me answering time and again, that's my name. When they are done with school, we drive through the narrow channel of streets that connect our neighborhood to Rock Creek Park. The large swath of river and trees runs as vertabrae through the northwestern corridor of the city. Before gentrification, a dividing line between spacious Georgians, Colonials with ostentatious pillars, modular boxes with windows overlooking the park, and the more crowded duplexes and apartments across the park and the never-ending street hustle of Georgia Avenue.

*

We walked the same path every day that spring through a canopy of tulip trees and elms, which cast a halo of gauzy light. Bikes whizzed by, and once we stopped to watch a pair of pileated woodpeckers, feet gripping oaks as they hammered away. The skipping of rocks, training them in this most elementary of tasks. The sort of thing that time now affords us, arm angles and flicks of wrist, sending the stones skimming over the water, briefly taking flight. The schematics are mathematical, but a properly skipped rock, whirring through the air, dimpling the water, looks like nothing so much as magic.

Most days they seemed not to notice the sadness that threatened to engulf me. I had to remind them I was miserable.

Daddy is sad.

Is that why you were being mean today?

*

Paul, then Saul, was once called the Pharisee of Pharisees. The man largely responsible for the expansion of western Christianity from regional religion to worldwide monolith converted after the death of Christ.

"Who are you, Lord?" Saul asked.

"I am Jesus, whom you are persecuting," he replied. "Now get up and go into the city, and you will be told what you must do."

The men traveling with Saul stood there speechless; they heard the sound but did not see anyone. Paul got up from the ground, but when he opened his eyes, he could see nothing. So, they led him by the hand into Damascus. For three days, he was blind and did not eat or drink anything.

*

In those early ship-wrecked days of sadness, I lashed myself to the mast of *Mad Men*. Don Draper, Madison avenue icon of glitz and glamour, consumption, and the immense emptiness of the hoary old American dream. Played by Jon Hamm, Draper is immaculate, thickly gelled hair held stiffly in place while he commands his subordinates, holds a boardroom in his thrall, or manipulates the women he loved. Don's charm and charisma overlay a moral tale about the fantasies we've all spun about our country, consumption and appearance above all else, but on a micro-level, what interested me was simple. Don was fucking unhappy.

The fascinating thing about Don is that he's vaguely aware of his unhappiness, but he's never able to change. He begins and ends the show as the same womanizing alcoholic who manically pursues success in the boardroom and bedroom as a means of fulfillment. There was never a question of his unhappiness; it was, in the way of friends I've had, so desperately obvious beneath the thin veneer of his smile. Instead, one conceit of the show was built around Don never realizing that changing his external circumstances, houses, wives, jobs, was ever going to shift his relationship to the world, never bring him that elusive thing, contentment. To quote the character: "But what is happiness? It's a moment before you need more happiness."

Whether Don is addicted to sex, alcohol, work, or himself, is mostly beside the point. Either way, there is something wrong at Don's core, which was either caused by his traumatic childhood in a brothel and subsequent terrifying experience in the war, or he's just a soulless asshole. The diagnosis largely depends on your feelings about personal vs. societal responsibility for outcomes and perhaps even the role of free will. The answer isn't remotely clear to me. And despite what you often read on Twitter, morality isn't as fixed or simple as purists would have you believe. In short, life is complex.

To the credit of the show, Don does experiment with change. He's briefly sober, briefly faithful, briefly not into his job, but he's always wedded to his unhappiness, his wandering and restless American fervor, which at breaking points, drives him west. Out west, the land of gold rush and new beginnings, Don reconnects with some lost self, his old life, his goodness. Then he returns home, and the change or attempt fades. He's doomed to return to the patterns of adultery, booze, and workaholic nature because that's his core character, deeply flawed.

*

For much of human history, it was supposed that the fates were what drove our destinies. Yes, people could be evil or deeply flawed, but they were also detritus washed up on the shores of fate, victims of circumstances beyond their control, the cruelty of the gods. What choice did Oedipus have? None. Is our character immutable, fixed at birth, or molded by the course of events outside our control? The contemporary critics would mostly say no, would mostly attribute morality to personal choice.

A zebra can't change its stripes.

Flamingo, Flamingo, what do you hear? I hear a zebra braying in my ear.

I got the braying right. I said the word braaay, extending it out in, what I can only describe as horsey a way as possible.

I identified with Don. To be clear, way less handsome, but I remembered the exact moment an existential hole opened beneath me. I was twenty-five, still fairly new to marriage, working at a thankless job shelving applications at a business school in Michigan. The sky was a grey lid, and the air was bone-chilling. Around me, I saw cold stone, salt lining the sidewalks. The birds had retreated from the bare husks of trees, which, to a native Californian, looked like kindling for the end of the world. I had my iPod on, and a sad song was playing, laced through with harmonica, and I will always remember that feeling of blasted desolation, the reality that you can't be anything as my teachers had told me, that adult life was a sham.

Over the years I tried to break through the malaise. I tried reading the classics, Garcia Marquez, Tolstoy, Woolf. I tried aesthetic experiences and typical distractions, writing, parenting, travel, intellectualizing, drinking, flirting, after a long time, fucking. But if these things seemed to briefly lift the veil, to offer a glimmer of hope, for a month, a golden year, they too would fade, turn into another disappointment.

The world is not interested in my happiness. The world is just the world. Everyone is a stranger here, from butterflies to blades of grass.

A human is a process, a system of inputs. Change the inputs, change the person. Without the ability to change, to form new neural connections, we'd roughly have the life of our ancestral sea slugs. In fact, it's our ability to adapt and change that makes much of our culture possible. Is change easy? No. Impossible. Only for the cynic. Rilke's "Archaic Torso of Apollo" does not end, You should probably change your life if change was possible. Good luck asshole! It ends:

> You must change your life.

The truth is, I hadn't been happy in a hell of a long time. But I wasn't sure happiness wasn't bullshit anyway. The sort of thing you chase after instead of reckoning with the reality of life, which is despair. Wouldn't I rather embrace the discordant reality of failed dreams, war, famine, and lies than embrace false happiness? At least I was living authentically, caressing the sound of a distant train whistle, the crack of winter ice, the long gaze into the middle distance.

*

I remembered leafing through the Sears catalog as a child, choosing between the GI Joe Helicopter or a realistic Transformer. Imagining the toy was sweeter than playing with it ever could be. Back then, you could connect my dreams for another life to the smell of new pages coming from the magazine.

My children make lists of things they want, rainbow corns and video games. How much of our desire is pulled from the cultural ether, from the relentless beautiful pictures of beautiful people in beautiful places, from the open kitchens to the Montessori schools and articles about parenting, finding romance, satisfaction, articles about having it all? Will my children imbibe the same unhappiness, hear the same stories about how the world will fulfill them and end in disappointment?

The truth is, my unhappiness, like Don's, wasn't something I was interested in giving up. It felt like an essential part of my core that I'd won through disappointment and intellectual application. I had always wanted things to be magical; the fact that they weren't and my disappointment at that reality, wasn't it a strange sense of hope? I'd never be any happier because I was constitutionally created for unhappiness. The Delphic oracle had spoken at my birth or at least at my high school graduation.

It's true, I should say. We do all have a happiness set point. I prefer the term well-being, which has less cultural baggage. However, it turns out those busy neural networks can be manipulated to modify our set point, increase our well-being. Hell, the Epicureans and Stoics were onto some of these tricks like negative visualization more than two thousand years ago. Those long walks, podcasts and meditation lead me to this sudden insight. Change was possible. The question became how?

*

Long before Christ, the Buddha sat under a tree and attained enlightenment. If Buddhism was anything like Jesus, I wasn't buying. But all I had to do at first was sit quietly too.

I sat in my room and stared at the blank wall. In the silence, I found a tumult of thought. The deep well turned up a surprising insight: my mind was batshit crazy. I couldn't pause for a second without recurrent thoughts popping in like an annoying neighbor. The mere suggestion of a pause, of reflection, sent me into a panic that had characterized my adult life. Without movement, without a magazine article, an online conversation, a flirtation, there was the endless abyss of existence that must be blotted out in order to obscure that existential hole threatening to swallow me. Life lacked meaning.

To paraphrase Tolstoy, happy people are all alike, unhappy people are unhappy in their own way. Is a story about changing for the better even worth telling? Or is that just my old intellectualism stopping by to assure me unhappiness is morally justified in the face of a world of injustice. Should I follow the objection to its logical conclusion?

*

"It is strange how much you can remember about places like that once you allow your mind to return into the grooves which lead back." —E.B. White

*

Habit change is difficult, neuroscientists agree. The grooves laid down guide us on familiar paths, welcome us back to familiar rooms, to see the things that brought us a reward, even if it only lasted a moment, and we woke up in ruin.

After I started meditation, I diverged from the neighborhood walks to enter the woods, green light slanting through the oaks, box elders, sycamores with carvings in them by now distant lovers. Raul and Monica '88. The air began to turn again from the crisp spring into the heaviness that characterizes an East Coast summer. I wept daily for the first time in my life. I sat on the edges of the creek or on the cushion of my yoga mat and cried. Sometimes they were soft tears leaking out from the corners of my eyes, but often, they were the sort of torrents of tears people call an ugly cry, my face crumpling, and deep wracking sobs shaking my body.

I was depressed for a month. I slept five hours a night, meditated for two or three hours a day, shepherded the kids through the day, with sandwiches and easy-to-cook dinners, and took long walks in the woods, and cried more. A month passed in this way, a direct reckoning with the choices in my life that had led to this crossroads, and it wasn't pretty.

The kids and I would walk together, and I'd hug them close to me, remind them I loved them. On days I didn't have them, I'd read books about Buddhism, responsibility, radical acceptance, or listen to *Happiness Lab* podcasts. I stopped the idle dating that had taken much of my free time. Suddenly, as though clouds were parting, it became clear I was the one who had made the proverbial bed and would have to lie in it. I cried. I asked for forgiveness. I forgave. I visualized an endless array of mistakes and of slights and wept.

The whole month was manic and a deep reset.

Post-traumatic growth, like change, is also a neurological reality, and I understood I'd need to embrace different habits of mind and life if I wanted to chase that elusory happiness. I had always been impulsive, impatient, easily irritable, and I'd seen similar characteristics torpedo my father's life and now mine. Whether that be infidelity or pure unpleasantness, the habits or actions were leading to the very unhappiness I thought was an inescapable reality.

*

Primates suffer through midlife crises as well. Something about the horizon of death shifts our perceptions, and we are given a moment, a pause to decide if the life we've chosen is the one we want. In the middle of life's road, I found myself in a dark wood.

In *Mad Men*, Don's crisis doesn't lead to any meaningful change. Instead, his restlessness and pursuit of attractive women and work at the expense of connection smacks of that American despair I felt on the walk home decades ago. Is this all there is? Just the flecks of light on water?

Most people start meditating because they've hit rock bottom, have suffered enough. That was true for me. There is no sexy way to describe sitting for an hour a day, trying to learn to identify thoughts and emotions as they arise, to slowly tend to whatever is left of your loving heart.

The ancient Greeks thought philosophy was a necessary part of a model for living a good life. Whether that was the Stoics, Seneca, and the emperor Marcus Aurelius, the garden school of Epicurus, founded on the idea of simplicity and friendship, or the followers of Aristotle, what was essential, was considering how a person should live.

During the Tang Dynasty in China, a period of cultural and artistic flowering, nearly every person in society, high and low, practiced Zen. In America, we venerate football, flag, and above all, power and fame. Thus, running beneath the current of the American dream is something hollow, a promise that the only way to live a good life is just over the next hill, another million, another contract, a little further west. The journey is never inward.

*

"I felt in need of a great pilgrimage, so I sat still for three days."
—Hafiz

*

The fundamental insight of my meditation was that suffering was a guarantee, as inescapable as plentiful light on the fields come summer. There wasn't some other life for me free of diapers and electric bills, scheming landlords and car insurance. This was life. The job was to be with it, to countenance it. Yes, to shift it, to change, but first, to not wish it away.

It's embarrassing for an intellectual sort to talk about self-love, but it was a road out of the dark woods into which I'd traveled. Learning to love whatever it was that I am, gave me the hope to shift, to change.

At the end of *Mad Men*, Don reaches the ultimate terminus, the state in which I grew up, California. He sits, beatific, on the coast, face bathed in light in a large group meditation. In *Mad Men*, the inner peace reflected in Jon Hamm's gorgeous face is an illusion, one more idea to commodify. The viewer knows Don's experience will be translated into an iconic Coke commercial. The gold rush of life.

*

When I was a child, my family would take vacations to the northern coast of California. We were poor after my father left, and a three-hour drive to the remote coast was all we could afford. In Fort Bragg, huge rocky outcroppings were pounded by the sea, sending water splashing into the air, while the wind whipped off the water, and above hung a low grey sky. Far above, the coast had redwoods, monoliths overlooking the sea, planted eons ago, by the province of wind and water, rocky soil and inland fog. Everything is native to somewhere else, even the earth used to be but a small point in the universe, waiting to be born, molten lava, nickel and iron, oxygen and carbon. Nothing but elements, waiting to change.

We stayed in a low-slung motel there, a single story that stretched the whole length of the cliff. In the afternoons, during rare sprays of sunlight, we'd toss the football on a large field of grass, running quick slants and post routes through flowers and molehills. When we were bored, we'd scrabble down the cliffs, feet slipping, and watch the waves hammer the shore. We built castles, but they were destroyed almost immediately in the icy froth. There was something almost contemplative in the sound, in the immediacy of the waves, the voracious winds, something of the indifference to us, to all our clamoring and fears, a reminder of our insignificance, which I associate with calm.

In the first year of my twelve-year marriage, my wife and I lived in a small studio, whose imperfect foundations made it a refuge for spiders that spun webs in every corner and hollow for the cool ocean breeze. Some nights I'd leave the studio and walk to the beach, threading my way through the quiet streets, cars parked here and there, windshields limned in salt. At the dead-end street two blocks away, I crossed the train tracks and through a small Eucalyptus grove until I reached the edge of the cliffs that overlooked the ocean. Then I'd sit quietly. I'd breathe in and out, wind ruffling my hair. In the distance, the moon lay across the Pacific as a lover, silvery threads tending to the dark endless ache of the ocean. In the distance, blocks away, was my new wife. I was alone with the ocean.

*

The other day when the children were with me, we witnessed a robin's furtive movements in the bushes, then a mad flapping and the wild spearing of the dirt until he'd grabbed the flailing body of a large worm.

Remember that dead deer? my son asked.

The body half-opened, innards displayed, reddened guts lying across a log where the children often played. We'd only spotted it after going over to play in the shallows, flies buzzing in its ribs.

I do, I answered.

When do you think I'll die?

Not for a very long time, son. But we'll all die someday, every step we take is in a place where something has once died, a worm, a sea slug, a beetle, an ant.

Stop talking about death, daddy.

It's the only certainty in life.

*

Ten months after the breakup and several months after the depression has lifted, I stand by Rock Creek, alone. It's winter, and the trees are emptied now; the winds and rain have scattered the leaves. The river is a ribbon of light passing through the small valley, and those trees hold up through their bare branches an electric blue sky.

I think of David Whyte, his beautiful poem, "Coleman's Bed." The final stanza, like a rhythm and a reminder all through those dismal months:

> Live in this place as you were meant to and then, surprised by your abilities, become the ancestor of it all, the quiet, robust and blessed Saint that your future happiness will always remember.

I made my way down those rocks from eons ago, sedimentary rocks from the Laurel formation, formed by volcanic ash before humans were even a twinkle in the eyes of evolution. I'm careful as I walk, such a fragile thing, a knee, a body, a life. Then I sit, crossing my legs, while the golden light washes the river, and I meditate. I think of that sense of awareness that runs as bedrock beneath the pandemonium of life. Sometimes I think there is something of those California days left inside me, as inside Don, a place I can quietly go. Is this a cliche? Have I become dense and easy to please in middle age? I don't know.

The truth is, I don't particularly care. I grip now, as tightly as I can, the edges of well-being for the first time in my adult life. The children and I read books again together every night, after we meditate. We tell each other about the things that have made us grateful during our days. We huddle together in my small bed and read until they are near sleep. I am trying to hold on to that feeling through meditaton, podcasts, books, the stoics. Perhaps I hold on so dearly because life in its vertiginous bounty, bell-shaped droplets hung from trees, bells of laughter from a friend, bells calling me back to meditation, all toll the same thing. Life is dear: Hold it, I tell myself. Hold it.

Acknowledgements (I)

Writing a book is a solitary act, but the material for the book particularly when it's an essay collection, are indebted to the people in the writer's life. To that end, I am first thankful to my children, Sadie and Julian, without whom my life would be infinitely less rich and interesting. A lot of these essays deal with wonders, difficulties and bafflements of raising little humans, and I am infinitely glad to be their father. These essays also wouldn't be possible without the support of my mother, who instilled an absolute love of reading in each of her children. Without that love, I am certain I never would have tried to become a writer.

Because these essays deal with a difficult period in my life, I am also thankful to my former spouse, who supported me through graduate school and has been a good co-parent as we've shepherded our kids from babies to teens. I am also thankful for my father, my brother, and my sister, who have helped to shape the writer, thinker, and person that I am.

I am thankful to the D.C. Commission on the Arts and Humanities for their grant, which has helped this project in its final stages. I am also deeply appreciative for the friendships, longtime and new, which have helped to sustain and mold me as a person, which is where the art comes from. Last, I want to thank my wife, Lauren, who is an absolute delight to partner with through the rocky shoals of life. I wouldn't have it any other way.

Acknowledgements (II)

"A Plane Crashes Over the Atlantic" appeared at *Hobart*

"A Field of White" appeared at *The Forge Literary Magazine*

"An Impressionist Sketch of a Saturday Afternoon" appeared at *Sou'wester*

"The Thin Ribbon" appeared at *The Chattahoochee Review*

"Time Passes: On Unfinished Things" appeared at *Post Road* and was listed as notable in B*est American Essays 2023*

"Departures" appeared at *The Manifest Station*

"On Trains" appeared at *Green Mountains Review*

"On Eating Animals" appeared at *The Crab Orchard Review*

"On Uncertainty" appeared at *Cimmaron Review*

"On Being 35" appeared at *Eclectica Magazine*

"On Showering and Mortality" appeared at *The ThreePenny Review*

"On Baths" appeared at *Hunger Mountain Review*

"This Essay Is About Everything" appeared at *Eclectica Magazine*

"Home Burial" appeared at *The Chattahoochee Review*

"The Leopard" appeared at *Mount Hope Magazine*

About the Author

Andrew Bertaina is the author of the short story collection *One Person Away From You* (2021), which won the Moon City Short Fiction Award. He has an MFA from American University in Washington, D.C., where he currently lives with his wife and four children. You can find more of his work at andrewbertaina.com.

— also from Autofocus Books —

Duplex — Mike Nagel

XO — Sara Rauch

Until It Feels Right — Emily Costa

Cleave — Holly Pelesky

Nextdoor in Colonialtown — Ryan Rivas

Too Much Tongue — Adrienne Marie Barrios & Leigh Chadwick

Picture Window — Danny Caine

the nature machine! — Tyler Gillespie

A Kind of In-Between — Aaron Burch

How to Write a Novel: An Anthology of 20 Craft Essays About Writing, None of Which Ever Mention Writing — ed. Aaron Burch

Hiraeth — Mistie Watkins

That Spell — Tate N. Oquendo

My Modest Blindness — Russell Brakefield

A Calendar Is A Snakeskin — Kristine Langley Mahler

Culdesac — Mike Nagel

Razed by TV Sets — Jason McCall

In the Away Time — Kristen E. Nelson